Japanese for Busy People I

Japanese for Busy People I

The Workbook

For The Revised 4th Edition

Association for
Japanese-Language Teaching
AJALT

This icon ( ) means that there is free audio available. To download these contents, search for "Japanese for Busy People" at kodansha.us.

The Association for Japanese-Language Teaching (AJALT) was recognized as a nonprofit organization by the Ministry of Education in 1977. It was established to meet the practical needs of people who are not necessarily specialists on Japan but who wish to communicate effectively in Japanese. In 1992 AJALT was awarded the Japan Foundation Special Prize. In 2010 it became a public interest incorporated association. AJALT maintains a website at www.ajalt.org.

Published by Kodansha USA Publishing, LLC, 451 Park Avenue South, New York, NY 10016

Distributed in the United Kingdom and continental Europe by Kodansha Europe Ltd.

First published in Japan in 1993 by Kodansha International
Fourth edition 2022 published by Kodansha USA, an imprint of Kodansha USA Publishing

Printed in Italy
25 24 23 22 5 4 3 2 1

ISBN: 978-1-56836-621-0

Editorial supervision by Kodansha Editorial, Ltd.
Editing and DTP by Guild, Inc.
Illustrations by Shinsaku Sumi and Kaori Ikeda
Cover design by Masumi Akiyama

Audio narration by Yoko Ibe, Fumiaki Kimura, Shogo Nakamura, Asahi Sasagawa, Yuji Suzuki, Ai Tanaka, and Hiroaki Tanaka
Audio recording and editing by the English Language Education Council, Inc.

Photo credits: © さるとびサスケ /PIXTA, 1. © レイコ /PIXTA, 1. © iStock.com/Yongyuan Dai, 1.

www.kodansha.us

CONTENTS

INTRODUCTION

Aims

This Workbook is designed to meet the needs of students who have studied Japanese but cannot yet speak it comfortably. It can be used both in and outside the classroom, in tandem with *Japanese for Busy People I, Revised 4th Edition*, or as material for independent study. It can also provide a good review for learners who have completed the equivalent of the first half of a typical first-year course but are not satisfied with their speaking ability. In short, it is fit for all beginning learners who wish to improve their speaking skills, regardless of their learning environment.

Features of the Workbook

Abundant Exercises

This Workbook contains an abundance of exercises following the topics of study introduced in each lesson of *Japanese for Busy People I, Revised 4th Edition*. The practice is diverse, extending from basic exercises to review and confirm vocabulary and conjugation to application of various forms of conversational style. Conversational skill can be acquired not only by understanding grammar and vocabulary but by practice through oral repetition. This Workbook can help you advance your mastery of Japanese.

Enjoyable Practice Using Audio Recordings and Illustrations

Practicing the dialogues may not be effective without some means for sensing them in reality. This workbook provides conversation practice using the most complex applications of the Exercises in the *Japanese for Busy People I, Revised 4th Edition*, along with Speaking Practice and Target Dialogue, all accompanied by illustrations. The audio recordings of these conversations can be downloaded. Looking at the illustrations while listening to the recordings allows study with a sense of actual experience.

Listening Practice

In actual conversation, more important than speaking ability is listening ability–to be able to accurately understand what a conversation partner is saying. This Workbook also focuses on cultivating the learner's listening comprehension. It includes dictation practice for the Target Dialogue and some Speaking Practice sections of each lesson.

Easy Independent Practice

When studying independently, the learner may not always benefit from the presence of a conversation partner to practice with. This Workbook also provides audio with blanks for the dictation parts so that one can practice the conversations even without a partner. By joining the conversations as if taking the part of the character, the learner can master the rhythms and timing of natural Japanese conversation.

Answers Download

The answers for all the Practice items can be downloaded. The answers follow the content of the main textbook.

How to Use the Workbook

Like *Japanese for Busy People I, Revised 4th Edition*, this Workbook is composed of 10 units and 24 lessons. Each lesson includes a number of Practice items, one to three Speaking Practice items, and a Target Dialogue. Some lessons include a Challenge page with slightly more advanced content. Review pages are provided after every two units. The Workbook ends with a Comprehensive Review page.

Practice

Each lesson in this Workbook has two main categories of Practice.

I. Practice without Audio Recording

One or two of the Practice items at the beginning of each lesson are for basic practice. They include practice to help fix vocabulary and conjugations in memory and to create short sentences and conversations while looking at the illustrations. Practice while following the instructions.

II. Practice with Audio Recording

Each lesson has Practice items with both illustrations and audio recordings. These are the conversation situations applying the most advanced content introduced in the Exercises in the main textbook. Please follow the following procedure for practice.

LESSON 1

PRACTICE ② 001

Make up a dialogue looking at the illustration. Then listen to the audio and check your work. Then practice by substituting the underlined words with words shown in the illustrations below.

Tanaka speaks to Brown, who he has just met for the first time.

Tanaka: 1 Sumimasen.
2 Rondon Ginkō no Buraun-san desu ka.
Buraun: 3 Hai, sō desu.

3

1) Read the situation text, look at the illustrations, and after grasping the situation pictured, follow the instructions and listen to the audio recording. Avoid looking at the script shown below the illustration and focus only on what you see in the illustration and hear on the recording. If you do not understand the conversation right away, keep looking and listening over and over until you do.

2) Now look at the script shown below the illustration.

3) Replicate the conversation one line at a time taking hints from the illustration and the words included in them. After trying to replicate the conversation without looking at the script, check the script to see if you have replicated it correctly.

4) Practice by listening to the recording and repeating consecutively or by shadowing until you can say all the lines in the script fluently.

5) Replace the part of the script that is underlined using information in the illustration as numbered below.

Speaking Practice

As in the Speaking Practice in the main textbook, the conversation situations are shown in the illustrations. Two patterns are given according to the nature of the conversation.

I. Practice by Dictation (the audio provides 2 tracks)

Practice the Speaking Practice in dictation format by the following steps.

LESSON 1
SPEAKING PRACTICE ③
006, 007
Listen to the audio while looking at the illustration and complete the dialogue.
Smith is visiting the Nozomi Department Store.
1. ABC Foods Smith
2. Tanaka-san, please.
3.
RECEPTION
Sumisu: 1 ABC Fūzu no Sumisu desu.
2 ( )
Uketsuke: 3 Hai.
5

1) Read the situation text, look at the illustrations, and after grasping the situation pictured, follow the instructions and listen to the audio recording. Avoid looking at the script shown below the illustration and focus only on what you see in the illustration and hear on the recording. If you do not understand the conversation right away, keep looking and listening over and over until you do.

2) Next, read the script to the right or below the illustration and write into the blank in parentheses the text as you have heard it.

3) Listen to the audio again and check whether your dictation is correct.

4) Practice by listening to the recording and repeating consecutively or by shadowing until you can say all the lines in the script fluently.

5) On the second track of the audio recording, pauses are provided for what was dictated on the first track. Practice saying those lines as if you are the character.

II. Practice by Substitution (audio provides one track)

Practice this style of Speaking Practice following the same steps as given on Practice with audio recording given on the previous page.

Target Dialogue
Practice all the Target Dialogues following the steps given for I. Practice by Dictation under Speaking Practice shown on the previous page.

Review
Review pages are provided after every two units. Practice by making sentences and dialogues using the vocabulary and sentence patterns practiced. Try to make the conversation in Japanese, looking at the illustrations and taking hints from the English provided.

Listening and Speaking Practice Techniques

Please try the following techniques for effective listening and speaking practice when using the practice items accompanied with audio recordings.
Repetition: Listen to the audio one sentence at a time and repeat consecutively.
Shadowing: Shadow the recording, repeating the words slightly behind the audio, as in the case of simultaneous interpretation. It is important to accurately imitate the audio not only in pronunciation but accent and intonation.

Acknowledgments for *Japanese for Busy People I: The Workbook* (2nd edition, 1994)
This Workbook was prepared by Akiko Kajikawa and Junko Shinada, teachers at AJALT, with the advice of Shigeko Miyazaki, Miyako Iwami, and Haruko Matsui, and the assistance of Yoko Hattori, Hiroko Kuroda, and Harumi Mizuno, all of whom are AJALT teachers.

Acknowledgments for *Japanese for Busy People I: The Workbook for the Revised 3rd Edition*
This Workbook was supervised by Izumi Sawa and written by five AJALT instructors; Erino Ido, Yoshiko Okubo, Yuko Takami, Hirohiko Matsuoka, and Chikako Watanabe.
For illustrations, we would like to thank Shinsaku Sumi.

Acknowledgments for *Japanese for Busy People I: The Workbook for the Revised 4th Edition*
This Workbook was written by nine AJALT instructors; Reiko Sawane, Hisako Aramaki, Eiko Ishida, Soko Onishi, Yuka Tanino, Yuko Hashimoto, Yumiko Matsuda, Yasuko Yako, and Tomoko Waga. Preparation for this Workbook was assisted by a grant from the Shoyu Club.
We the authors would like to sincerely thank Shinsaku Sumi and Kaori Ikeda, our illustrators, for their lively and skillful pictures that bring the content of the lessons alive for students.
In the compilation of this revised edition, we would like to express our gratitude to Mio Urata of Kodansha Editorial and Makiko Ohashi of Guild, Inc. for their cooperation.

Audio and Answers Download

The audio and answers for this book can be downloaded to your smartphone, tablet, or PC, free of charge.

To download these contents, search for "Japanese for Busy People" at kodansha.us.

The audio files are in MP3 format and include Practice (partially), Speaking Practice, and Target Dialogue.

THE WORKBOOK

LESSON 1 Meeting: Nice to Meet You

PRACTICE ①

Make up dialogues following the patterns of the examples and based on the information provided.

1. & 2. e.g.

Smith
American

①

Hoffman
German

②

Brown
British

③

Chan
Chinese

④

Raja
Indian

⑤

Harris
Australian

⑥

Emma
French
[Furansu-jin]

⑦

Tanaka
Japanese

1. e.g. A: Sumisu-san wa Amerika-jin desu ka.
B: Hai, Amerika-jin desu.

2. e.g. A: Sumisu-san wa Ōsutoraria-jin desu ka.
B: Iie, Amerika-jin desu.

VOCABULARY

Furansu-jin	French person
Furansu	France

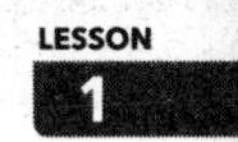

PRACTICE ②

001

Make up a dialogue looking at the illustration. Then listen to the audio and check your work. Then practice by substituting the underlined words with words shown in the illustrations below.

Tanaka speaks to Brown, who he has just met for the first time.

Tanaka: [1] **Sumimasen.**
[2] **Rondon Ginkō no Buraun-san desu ka.**

Buraun: [3] **Hai, sō desu.**

①
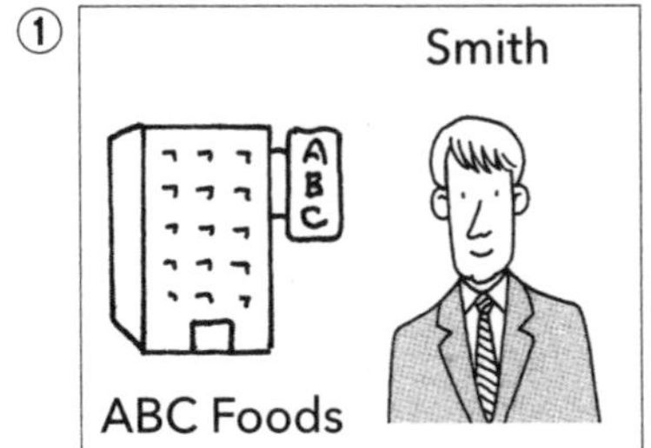

②
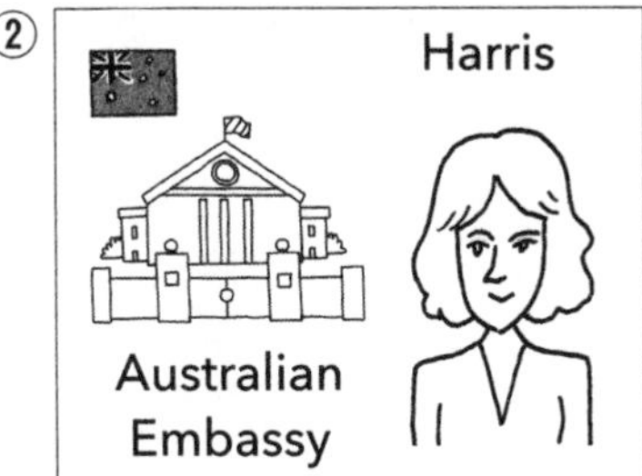

③

SPEAKING PRACTICE ①

Listen to the audio while looking at the illustration and complete the dialogue.
Tanaka and Smith, who have just met for the first time, are talking.

Tanaka: [1] (   )
Sumisu: [2] **Amerika desu.**

SPEAKING PRACTICE ②

Listen to the audio while looking at the illustrations and complete the dialogue.
Sasaki introduces Brown to Tanaka.

Sasaki: [1] (   )
Buraun: [2] **Hajimemashite.** [3] **Buraun desu.** [4] **Yoroshiku onegaishimasu.**
Tanaka: [5] (   )
[6] (   )
[7] (   )

SPEAKING PRACTICE ③

Listen to the audio while looking at the illustration and complete the dialogue.
Smith is visiting the Nozomi Department Store.

1.
ABC Foods
Smith

2.
Tanaka-san, please.

RECEPTION

3.

Sumisu: [1] **ABC Fūzu no Sumisu desu.**

[2] (   )

Uketsuke: [3] **Hai.**

TARGET DIALOGUE

 008, 009

Listen to the audio while looking at the illustrations and complete the dialogue.

Smith meets Tanaka for the first time. Tanaka is visiting ABC Foods.

1.

2. Nozomi Department Store Tanaka-san?

3.

4.

5. ABC Foods Smith

6.

7.

8. Tanaka

9.

Sumisu: [1] ( )

[2] ( )

Tanaka: [3] Hai, sō desu.

Sumisu: [4] ( )

[5] ( )

[6] ( )

Tanaka: [7] Hajimemashite.

[8] Tanaka desu.

[9] Kochira koso, yoroshiku onegaishimasu.

PRACTICE ①

Look at the illustration and make up sentences following the pattern of the example. Substitute the underlined part with the alternatives given.

e.g.

① のぞみデパート株式会社
食品部　部長
② 田中　真吾

③ 〒105-0001　東京都港区虎ノ門 3-25-2
④ TEL：03-3459-9620
携帯：090-8765-4321
⑤ s.tanaka@nozomidpt.com
https: //www.nozomidpt.jp/

Nozomi Ltd.
Shingo Tanaka
Manager, Foods Dept.

3-25-2 Toranomon Minato-ku, Tokyo 105-0001
Phone: 03-3459-9620
Mobile: 090-8765-4321
s.tanaka@nozomidpt.com
https: //www.nozomidpt.jp/

e.g. Kore wa <u>meishi</u> desu.

① kaisha no namae
② namae
③ jūsho
④ denwa-bangō
⑤ mēru-adoresu

PRACTICE ②

010

Make up a dialogue looking at the illustrations. Then listen to the audio and check your work. Then practice by substituting the underlined words with words shown in the illustrations below.

After a meeting, Smith finds a file, so he asks Suzuki about it.

1.
Suzuki
?
2.
No.
3.
?
4.
Emma-san's

Sumisu: 1 **Kore wa Suzuki-san no fairu desu ka.**
Suzuki: 2 **Iie, watashi no ja arimasen.**
Sumisu: 3 **Dare no desu ka.**
Suzuki: 4 **Ema-san no desu.**

①

②

SPEAKING PRACTICE ①

011

Listen to the audio while looking at the illustration. Then practice by substituting the underlined words with words shown in the illustrations below.

Smith finds something in the break room.

Sumisu: [1] **Kore wa nan desu ka.**
Nakamura: [2] **Nihon no o-kashi desu. Dōzo.**
Sumisu: [3] **Arigatō gozaimasu.**

① 
Hokkaidō no kukkī

② 
Chūgoku no o-kashi

VOCABULARY

Hokkaidō no kukkī	cookies from Hokkaido
Chūgoku no o-kashi	sweets from China

SPEAKING PRACTICE ②

Make up a dialogue looking at the illustration. Then listen to the audio and check yourself. Then practice by substituting the underlined words with words shown in the illustrations below.

Smith and Nakamura are working at the office.

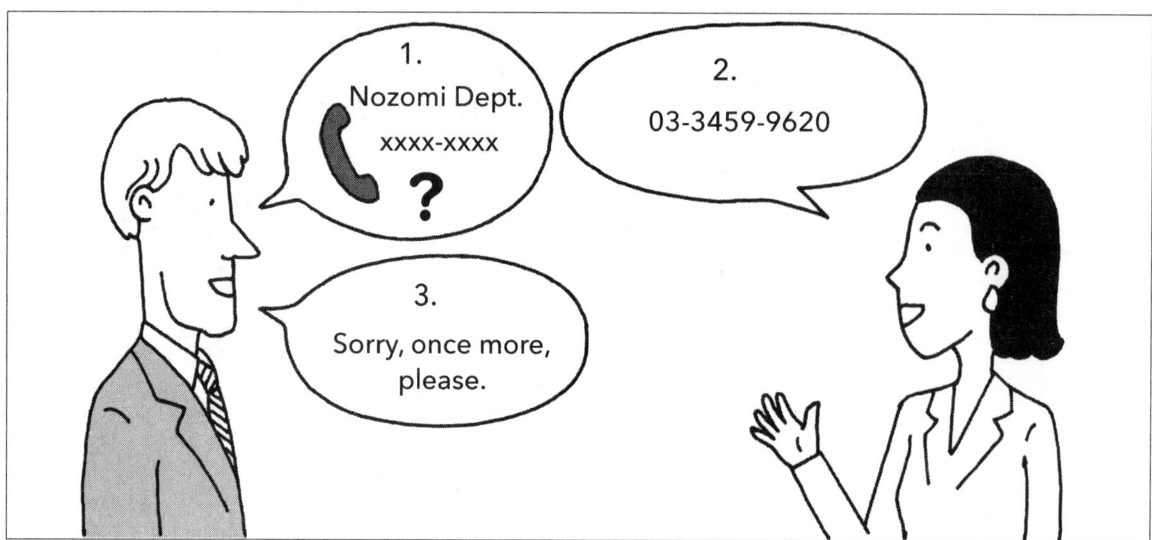

Sumisu: [1] **Nozomi Depāto no denwa-bangō o oshiete kudasai.**
Nakamura: [2] **03-3459-9620 desu.**
Sumisu: [3] **Sumimasen. Mō ichi-do onegaishimasu.**

① 

keisatsu 110

② 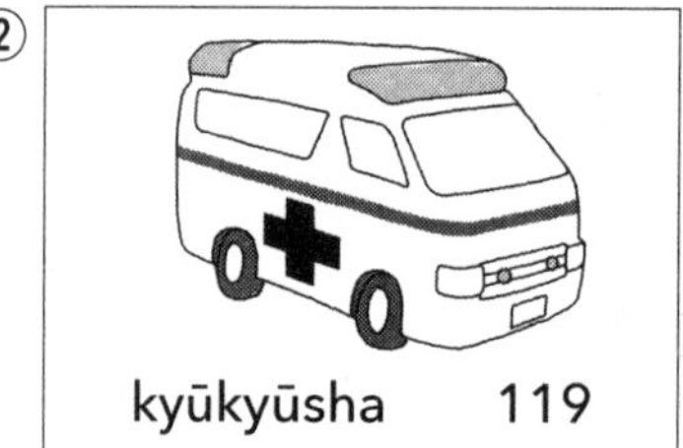
kyūkyūsha 119

VOCABULARY

keisatsu	police
kyūkyūsha	ambulance

TARGET DIALOGUE

013, 014

Listen to the audio while looking at the illustrations and complete the dialogue.

A meeting has just ended. Nakamura finds a pen on the floor.

Nakamura: [1] Kore wa dare no pen desu ka.

Suzuki: [2] Sā, wakarimasen.

[3] Sumisu-san no desu ka.

Sumisu: [4] (   )

Nakamura: [5] Tanaka-san, kore wa Tanaka-san no pen desu ka.

Tanaka: [6] (   )

[7] Arigatō gozaimasu.

Asking the Time: What Time Is It?

PRACTICE ①

1. Make up dialogues following the pattern of the example and based on the information provided.

e.g.	①	②	③
8:00	5:30	1:15	7:40

④	⑤	⑥	⑦
12:05	9:00	2:45	6:00

e.g. A: Ima nan-ji desu ka.
B: 8-ji desu.

2. Make up dialogues following the pattern of the example and based on the information provided.

e.g.	①	②	③
Pari 11:00 A.M.	Honkon 4:30 P.M.	Shanhai 3:00 P.M.	Sanfuran- shisuko 10:20 A.M.

④	⑤	⑥	⑦
Mirano 1:50 P.M.	Honoruru 8:30 P.M.	Shidonī 9:00 A.M.	Dobai 1:30 A.M.

e.g. A: Pari wa ima nan-ji desu ka.
B: Gozen 11-ji desu.

VOCABULARY

Pari	Paris	**Sanfuranshisuko**	San Francisco	**Shidonī**	Sydney
Honkon	Hong Kong	**Mirano**	Milan	**Dobai**	Dubai
Shanhai	Shanghai	**Honoruru**	Honolulu		

PRACTICE ②

Make up dialogues following the patterns of the examples and based on the information provided.

1. e.g.
department store
10:00–7:00

①
bank
9:00–3:00

②
supermarket
8:30 A.M.–9:00 P.M.

③
gym
7:00 A.M.–8:00 P.M.

④
work
9:00–5:00

⑤
lunchtime
11:30–2:30

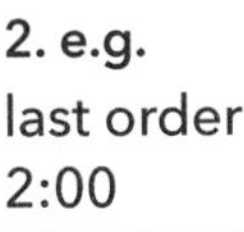

2. e.g.
last order
2:00

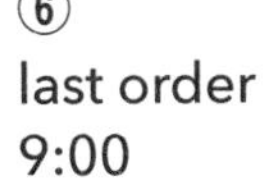

⑥
last order
9:00

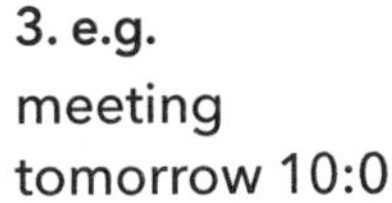

3. e.g.
meeting
tomorrow 10:00

⑦
party
today 7:00

1. e.g. **A: Depāto wa nan-ji kara desu ka.**
B: 10-ji kara desu.
A: Nan-ji made desu ka.
B: 7-ji made desu.

2. e.g. **A: Rasuto-ōdā wa nan-ji desu ka.**
B: 2-ji desu.

3. e.g. **A: Kaigi wa itsu desu ka.**
B: Ashita no 10-ji kara desu.

PRACTICE ③

015

Listen to the audio while looking at the illustration. Then practice by substituting the underlined words with words shown in the illustration below.

Chan is staying at a hotel. She asks about the hotel services.

Chan: [1] **Sumimasen. Ban-gohan wa nan-ji kara desu ka.**
Furonto: [2] **6-ji kara desu.**
Chan: [3] **Arigatō gozaimasu.**

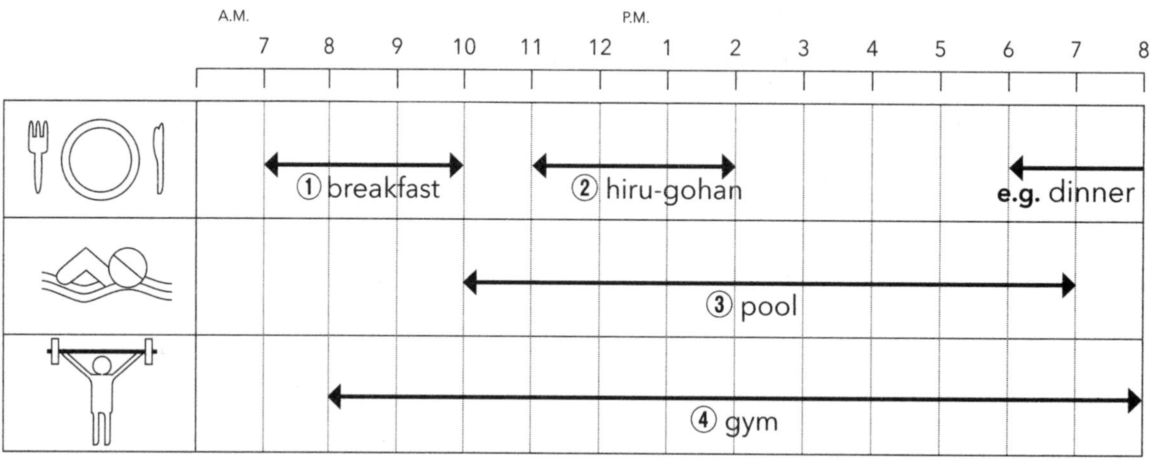

VOCABULARY

hiru-gohan	lunch

SPEAKING PRACTICE

016

Listen to the audio while looking at the illustrations. Then practice by substituting the underlined words with words shown in the illustrations below.

Sasaki wants to call the London branch of her company.

1. now ?
2. (clock)
3. London now ?
4. A.M.
5. Thank you.

Sasaki: [1] **Nakamura-san, ima nan-ji desu ka.**

Nakamura: [2] **4-ji han desu.**

Sasaki: [3] **Rondon wa ima nan-ji desu ka.**

Nakamura: [4] **Gozen 8-ji han desu.**

Sasaki: [5] **Sō desu ka. Dōmo arigatō.**

①

②
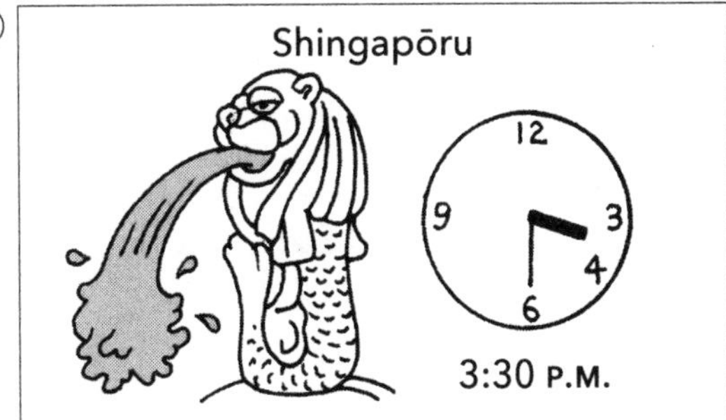

VOCABULARY

Nyūyōku	New York
Shingapōru	Singapore

TARGET DIALOGUE

017, 018

Make up a dialogue looking at the illustrations. Then listen to the audio and check yourself.
Smith is calling the "Sushiyoshi" sushi shop.

1. Sushiyoshi
2. lunch time from
3. from
4. until
5. until
6. last order
7.
8. Thank you.

Mise no hito: [1] **Sushiyoshi desu.**
Sumisu: [2] (　　　　　　　　　　　　　　　　　　　　　　　　　　　　)
Mise no hito: [3] **11-ji han kara desu.**
Sumisu: [4] (　　　　　　　　　　　　　　　　　　　　　　　　　　　　)
Mise no hito: [5] **2-ji han made desu.**
Sumisu: [6] (　　　　　　　　　　　　　　　　　　　　　　　　　　　　)
Mise no hito: [7] **2-ji desu.**
Sumisu: [8] (　　　　　　　　　　　　　　　　　　　　　　　　　　　　)

PRACTICE ①

Look at the illustration and state the price of each item.

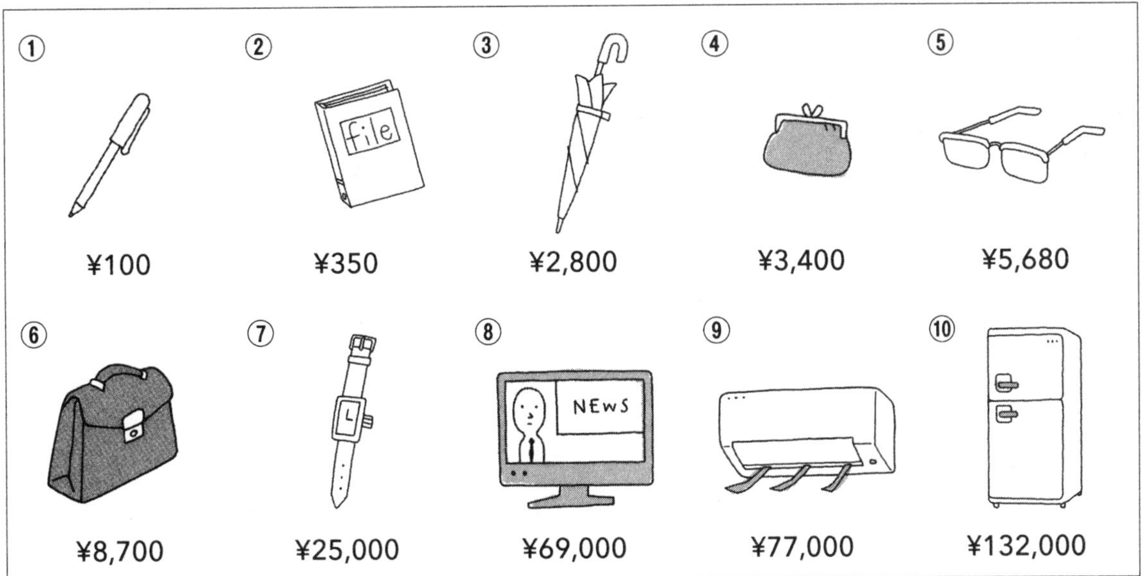

PRACTICE ②

Make up dialogues following the patterns of the examples and based on the information provided.

Smith is shopping in a recyle shop.

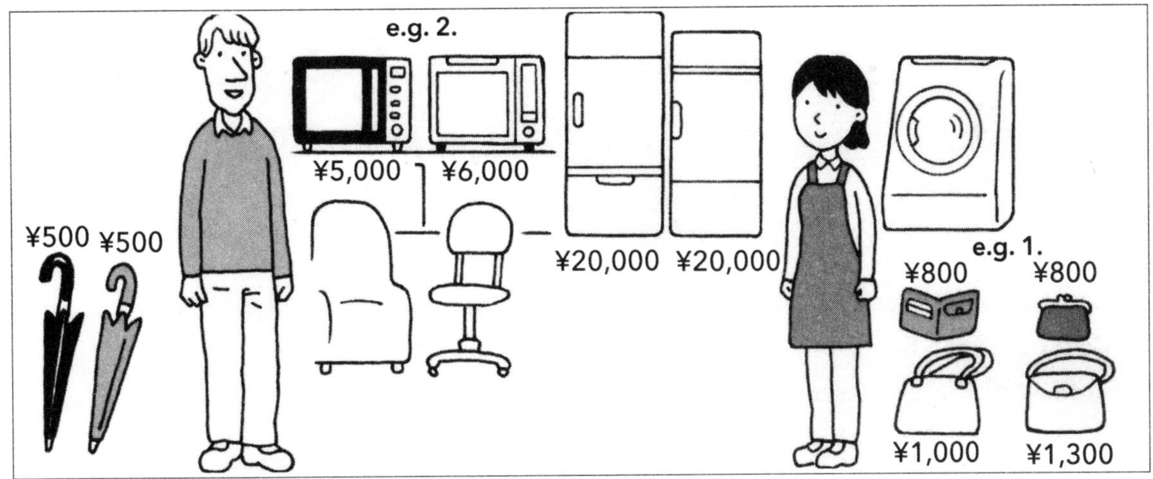

e.g. 1. Sumisu: Sore wa ikura desu ka.
Mise no hito: 800-en desu.
Sumisu: Sore mo 800-en desu ka.
Mise no hito: Hai, 800-en desu.

e.g. 2. Sumisu: Are wa ikura desu ka.
Mise no hito: 5,000-en desu.
Sumisu: Are mo 5,000-en desu ka.
Mise no hito: Iie, are wa 6,000-en desu.

PRACTICE ③

019

Listen to the audio while looking at the illustrations. Then practice by substituting the underlined words with words shown in the illustrations below.

Smith is at a store, shopping.

1. personal computer ?

2. No. tablet

3. personal computer ?

4. Yes.

5. ¥ ?

6. ¥40,000

7. I'll take it.

Sumisu: [1] Sumimasen. Are wa pasokon desu ka.
Mise no hito: [2] Iie, taburetto desu.
Sumisu: [3] Sore wa pasokon desu ka.
Mise no hito: [4] Hai, sō desu.
Sumisu: [5] Ikura desu ka.
Mise no hito: [6] 40,000-en desu.
Sumisu: [7] Ja, sore o kudasai.

①
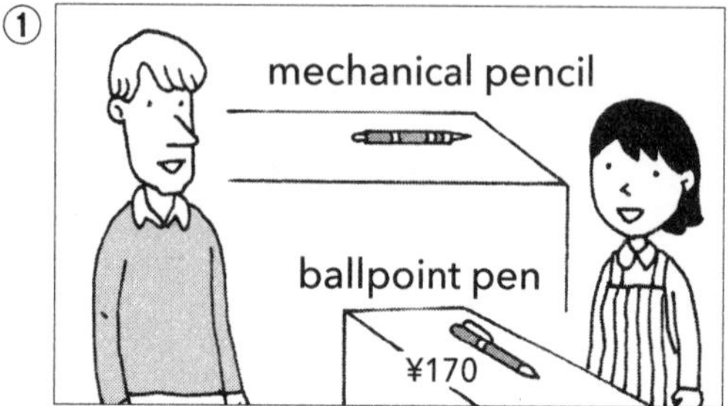

②
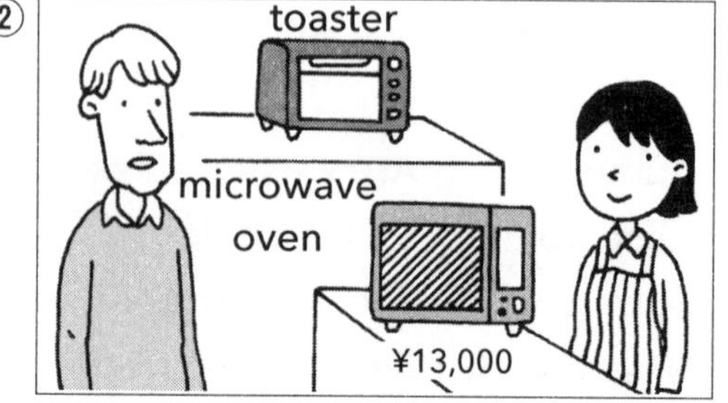

SPEAKING PRACTICE ①

020

Listen to the audio while looking at the illustration. Then practice by substituting the underlined words with words shown in the illustrations below.

Smith is placing his order at a coffee shop.

Sumisu: [1] **Sumimasen. <u>Sandoitchi to kōhī</u> o onegaishimasu.**

Mise no hito: [2] **Hai.**

① 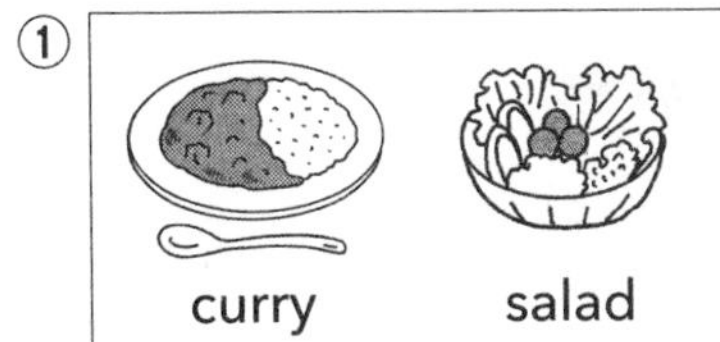

② 

SPEAKING PRACTICE ②

Listen to the audio while looking at the illustration and complete the dialogue.

Smith is shopping in a store.

Sumisu: [1] ( )

Mise no hito: [2] **8,300-en desu.**

Sumisu: [3] ( )

Mise no hito: [4] **Hai.**

TARGET DIALOGUE

Listen to the audio while looking at the illustrations and complete the dialogue.

Smith is shopping.

2. Please show me.

1.

4. Thank you.

5. ¥?

3.

6. ¥3,000

7. ¥?

8. ¥3,000

9. I'll take this.

10.

Mise no hito: [1] **Irasshaimase.**

Sumisu: [2] (   )

Mise no hito: [3] **Hai, dōzo.**

Sumisu: [4] (   )

[5] (   )

Mise no hito: [6] **3,000-en desu.**

Sumisu: [7] (   )

Mise no hito: [8] **Are mo 3,000-en desu.**

Sumisu: [9] (   )

Mise no hito: [10] **Hai, arigatō gozaimasu.**

CHALLENGE 1

025

Listen to the audio while looking at the illustration. Then practice by substituting the underlined words with words shown in the illustrations below.

Smith is shopping at the fish store.

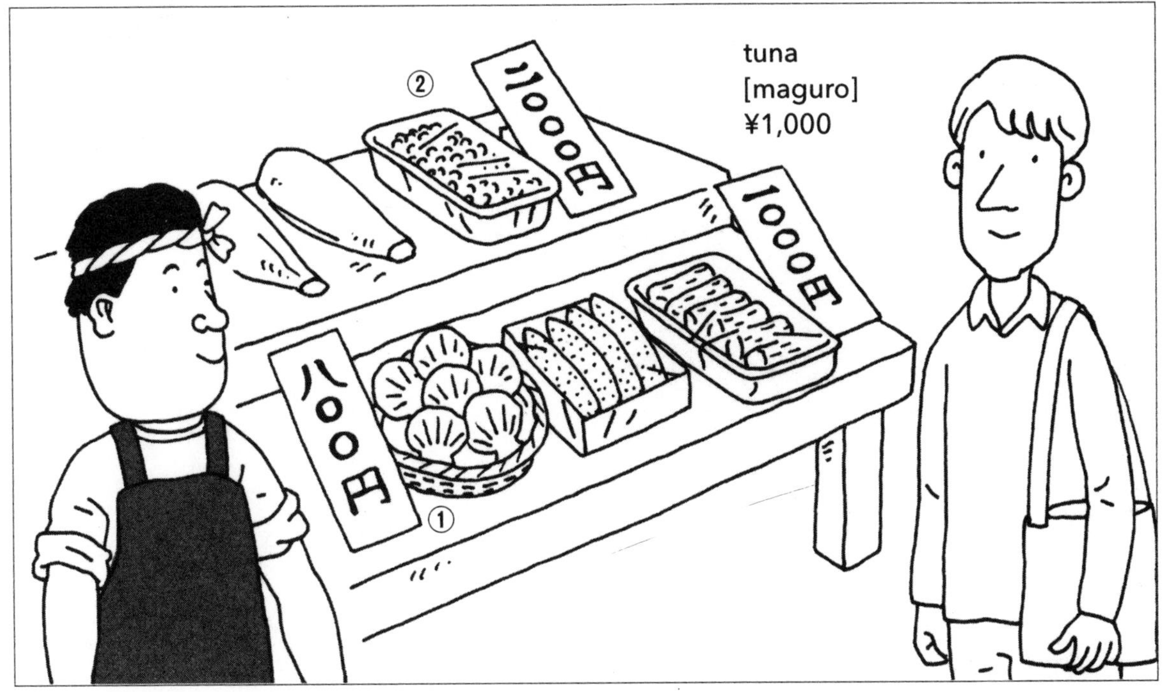

Mise no hito: Irasshaimase.
Sumisu: Kore wa nan desu ka.
Mise no hito: Maguro desu. "Tuna" desu.
Sumisu: Ikura desu ka.
Mise no hito: 1,000-en desu.
Sumisu: Ja, kore o kudasai.
Mise no hito: Reji-bukuro wa irimasu ka.
Sumisu: Iie, kekkō desu.

① 
hotate, "scallops"
¥800

② 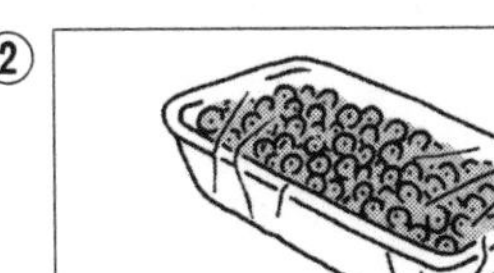
ikura, "salmon roe"
¥2,000

VOCABULARY

maguro	tuna	irimasu	need	hotate	scallops
reji-bukuro	shopping bag	Iie, kekkō desu.	No thank you.	ikura	salmon roe

Shopping (2): Two Bottles of That Wine, Please

PRACTICE ①

Fill in the blanks with the appropriate words.

	(plate, shirt) etc.	(bottle, umbrella) etc.	(apple, hamburger) etc.
1	ichi-mai	⑨	⑰
2	①	ni-hon	futatsu
3	②	⑩	⑱
4	③	⑪	yottsu
5	④	⑫	⑲
6	⑤	roppon	⑳
7	⑥	⑬	㉑
8	hachi-mai	⑭	㉒
9	⑦	⑮	㉓
10	⑧	⑯	tō

PRACTICE ②

Make up questions following the pattern of the example and based on the information provided.

Smith is shopping at a sundries store.

e.g. Sumisu: Kono akai sētā wa ikura desu ka.

VOCABULARY

bōshi	hat, cap	**kōto**	coat
nōto	notebook	**sētā**	sweater

PRACTICE ③

Listen to the audio while looking at the illustrations. Then practice by substituting the underlined words with words shown in the illustrations below.

Chan is shopping.

1. ¥?

2. ¥1,200

3. ?

4. Canada [Kanada]

5. x 3

Chan:	1 Sumimasen. Sono <u>bīru</u> wa ikura desu ka.
Mise no hito:	2 1,200-en desu.
Chan:	3 Sore wa doko no <u>bīru</u> desu ka.
Mise no hito:	4 <u>Kanada</u> no desu.
Chan:	5 Ja, sore o <u>3-bon</u> kudasai.

①
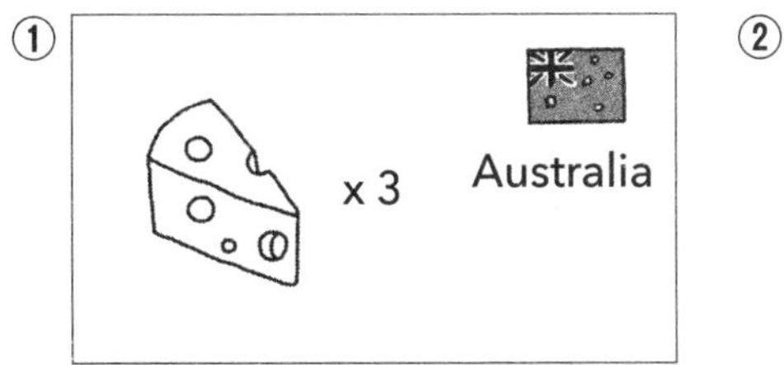

②
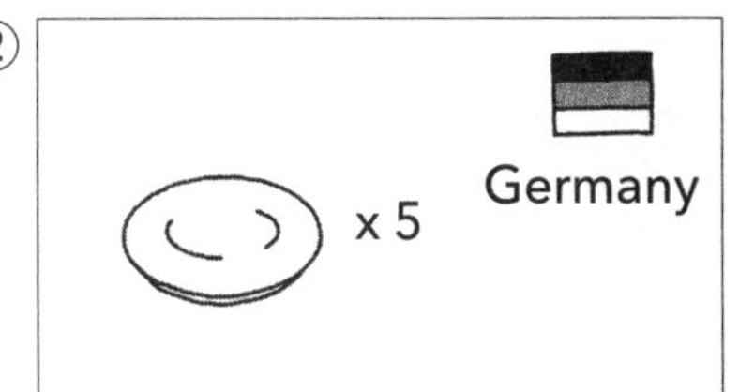

VOCABULARY

Kanada	Canada

SPEAKING PRACTICE ①

027

Listen to the audio while looking at the illustration. Then practice by substituting the underlined words with words shown in the illustrations below.

Smith is shopping in a clothing store.

Sumisu:	[1] Sumimasen. Ano T-shatsu wa ikura desu ka.
Mise no hito:	[2] Dore desu ka.
Sumisu:	[3] Ano aoi T-shatsu desu.
Mise no hito:	[4] 2,000-en desu.

①
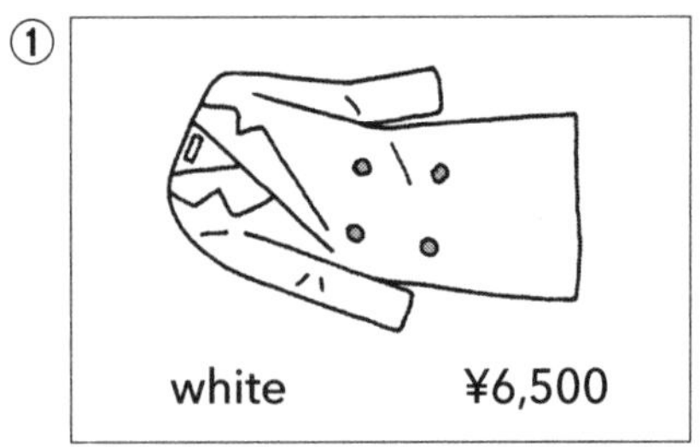

②

SPEAKING PRACTICE ②

 028, 029

Listen to the audio while looking at the illustration and complete the dialogue.

Chan is shopping in a cake shop.

Mise no hito: [1] **Irasshaimase.**

Chan: [2] **(**   **)**

Mise no hito: [3] **Hai. 2,500-en desu.**

SPEAKING PRACTICE ③

 030

Listen to the audio while looking at the illustration. Then practice by substituting the underlined word with words shown in the illustrations below.

Chan is asking something to a shopkeeper in a shopping mall.

Chan: [1] **<u>Otearai</u> wa doko desu ka.**

Mise no hito: [2] **Achira desu.**

Chan: [3] **Dōmo.**

①

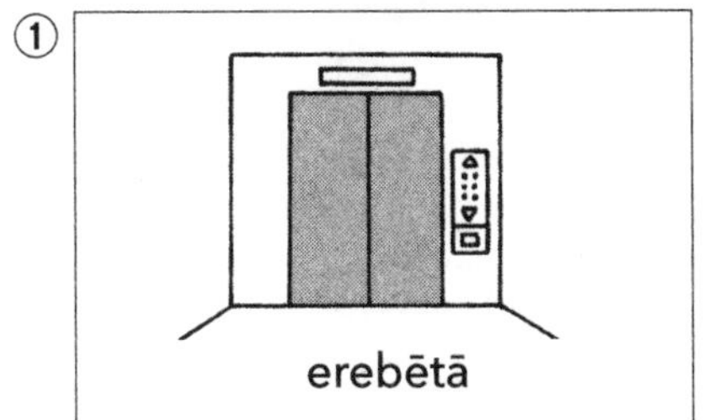

②

VOCABULARY

erebētā	elevator
o-kaikei	cashier's desk

TARGET DIALOGUE

 031, 032

Listen to the audio while looking at the illustrations and complete the dialogue.

Smith is at the information desk in a shopping mall.

1. Where?

? Information

2. B1F

3. Thank you.

4. ?

5. France

6. ¥?

7. ¥2,600

9. x 2, too

8. x 2

Sumisu: [1]( )

Infomēshon no hito: [2] Chika 1-kai desu.

Sumisu: [3]( )

Sumisu: [4]( )

Mise no hito: [5] Furansu no desu.

Sumisu: [6]( )

Mise no hito: [7] 2,600-en desu.

Sumisu: [8](

[9]( )

CHALLENGE 2

033

Listen to the audio while looking at the illustrations. Then practice by substituting the underlined words with words shown in the illustrations below.

Smith is ordering takeout at a fast food restaurant.

Mise no hito: [1] **Irasshaimase.**

[2] **Tennai de o-meshiagari desu ka.**

Sumisu: [3] **Iie, mochikaeri de.**

Mise no hito: [4] **Go-chūmon o dōzo.**

Sumisu: [5] **<u>Hanbāgā o futatsu to kōra o hitotsu kudasai.</u>**

①

②

③

VOCABULARY

kōra	cola	Go-chūmon o dōzo.	What would you like to order?
Tennai de o-meshiagari desu ka.	Will you have it here?	hanbāgā	hamburger
mochikaeri de	to go, please	poteto	French fries

REVIEW 1

Look at the illustration and make up a dialogue. Then practice by substituting the underlined words with words shown in the illustrations below.

Chan and Nakamura are attending a party.

1. Chairat-san

2.

3. ABC Foods Nakamura

4.

5.

6. Bangkok Airlines Chairat

7.

Chan: [1] **Kochira wa <u>Chairatto-san</u> desu.**

Nakamura: [2] **Hajimemashite.**

[3] **ABC Fūzu no Nakamura desu.**

[4] **Yoroshiku onegaishimasu.**

<u>Chairatto</u>: [5] **Hajimemashite.**

[6] **<u>Bankoku Kōkū no Chairatto</u> desu.**

[7] **Yoroshiku onegaishimasu.**

①

Harris
Australian Embassy

②

Takahashi
Nozomi Department Store

③

Ogawa
Bank of London

④

Kojima
JBP Japan

VOCABULARY

Chairatto	Chairat (surname)	Takahashi	Takahashi (surname)	Kojima	Kojima (surname)
Bankoku Kōkū	Bangkok Airlines (fictitious company name)	Ogawa	Ogawa (surname)	JBP Japan	JBP Japan (fictitious company nam

LESSON **6** # Going Places (1): Where Are You Going?

PRACTICE ①

Fill in the blanks with the appropriate words.

	Last	This	Next
day	①	kyō	②
week	senshū	③	④
month	⑤	⑥	⑦
year	⑧	⑨	⑩

PRACTICE ②

Make up sentences or dialogues following the patterns of the examples and based on the information provided.

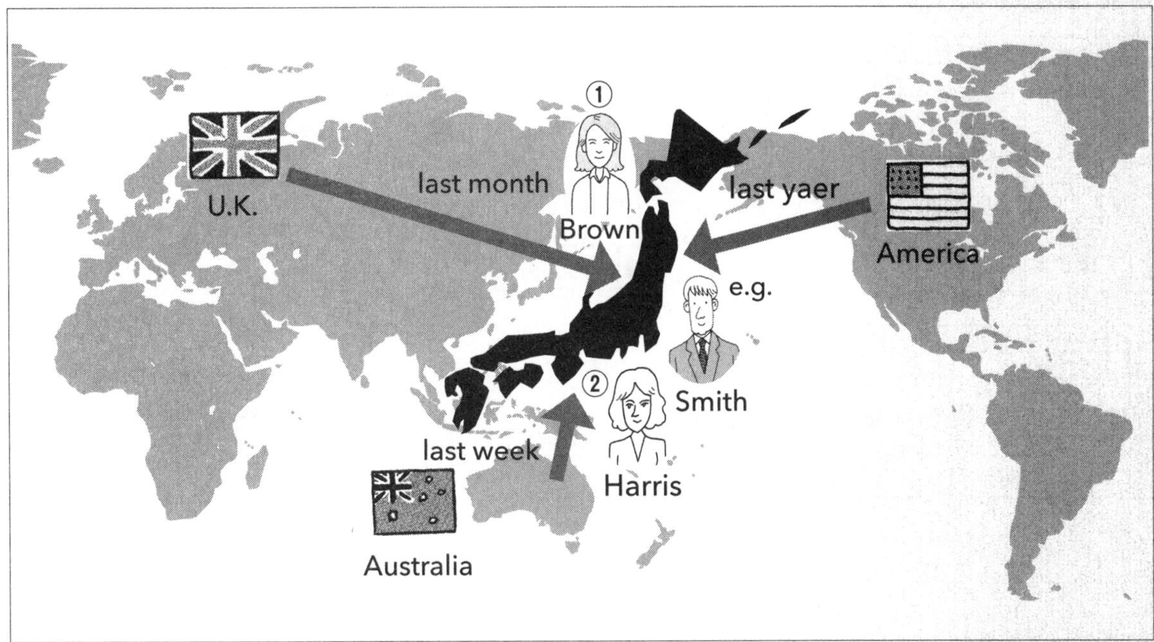

1. e.g. Sumisu-san wa kyonen Amerika kara Nihon ni kimashita.

2. e.g. A: Sumisu-san wa doko kara kimashita ka.
   B: Amerika kara kimashita.

3. e.g. A: Sumisu-san wa itsu Nihon ni kimashita ka.
   B: Kyonen kimashita.

PRACTICE ③

Make up sentences following the pattern of the example and based on the information provided.

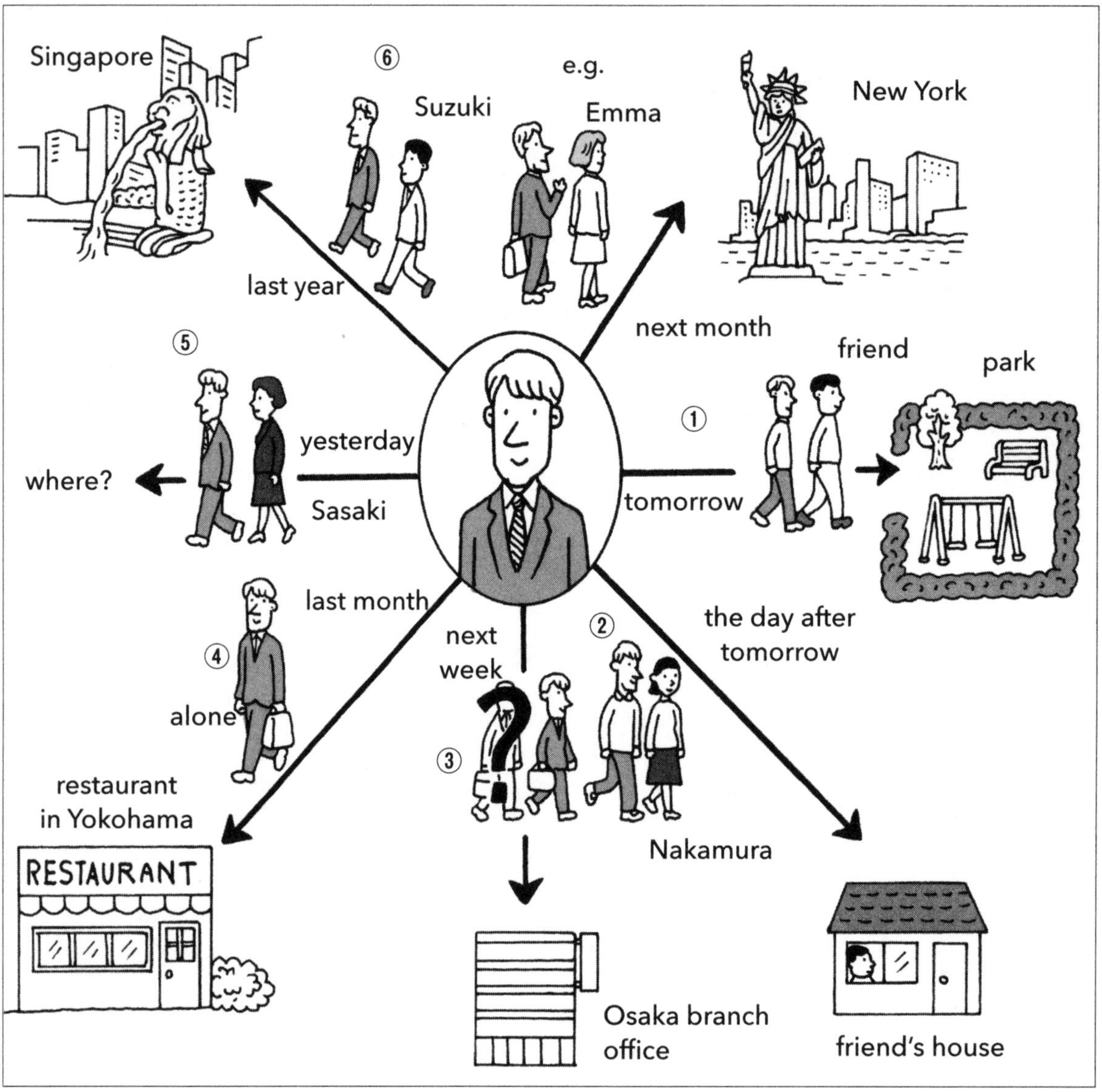

Singapore
⑥ Suzuki
last year
e.g. Emma
next month
New York
⑤
where?
yesterday
Sasaki
① friend
tomorrow
park
④ alone
last month
restaurant in Yokohama
RESTAURANT
next week
③
② Nakamura
Osaka branch office
the day after tomorrow
friend's house

e.g. Sumisu-san wa raigetsu Ema-san to Nyūyōku ni ikimasu.

PRACTICE ④

Listen to the audio while looking at the illustrations. Then practice by substituting the underlined words with words shown in the illustrations below.

Smith is talking on the phone with a person from the Yokohama branch office.

Yokohama branch
1.
when
2.
tomorrow
Yokohama branch office
Yokohama branch
3.
4.
Sasaki-san
5.

Yokohama-shisha no hito : [1] **Sumisu-san wa itsu Yokohama-shisha ni kimasu ka.**
Sumisu : [2] **Ashita ikimasu.**
Yokohama-shisha no hito : [3] **Dare to kimasu ka.**
Sumisu : [4] **Sasaki-san to ikimasu.**
Yokohama-shisha no hito : [5] **Sō desu ka.**

①

②

SPEAKING PRACTICE ①

035, 036

Listen to the audio while looking at the illustration and complete the dialogue.

From today, Raja is starting an internship at ABC Foods.

7.

1. intern Raja-san

2.

3. Raja

4. from India

5. University of Tokyo student

6.

Sasaki: [1] Kochira wa intān no Raja-san desu.

Raja: [2] Hajimemashite.

[3] Raja desu.

[4] (   )

[5] (   )

[6] (   )

Kaisha no hito-tachi: [7] Yoroshiku onegaishimasu.

SPEAKING PRACTICE ②

Listen to the audio while looking at the illustration. Then practice by substituting the underlined words with words shown in the illustrations below.

At a bus stop, Smith asks the driver a question before boarding.

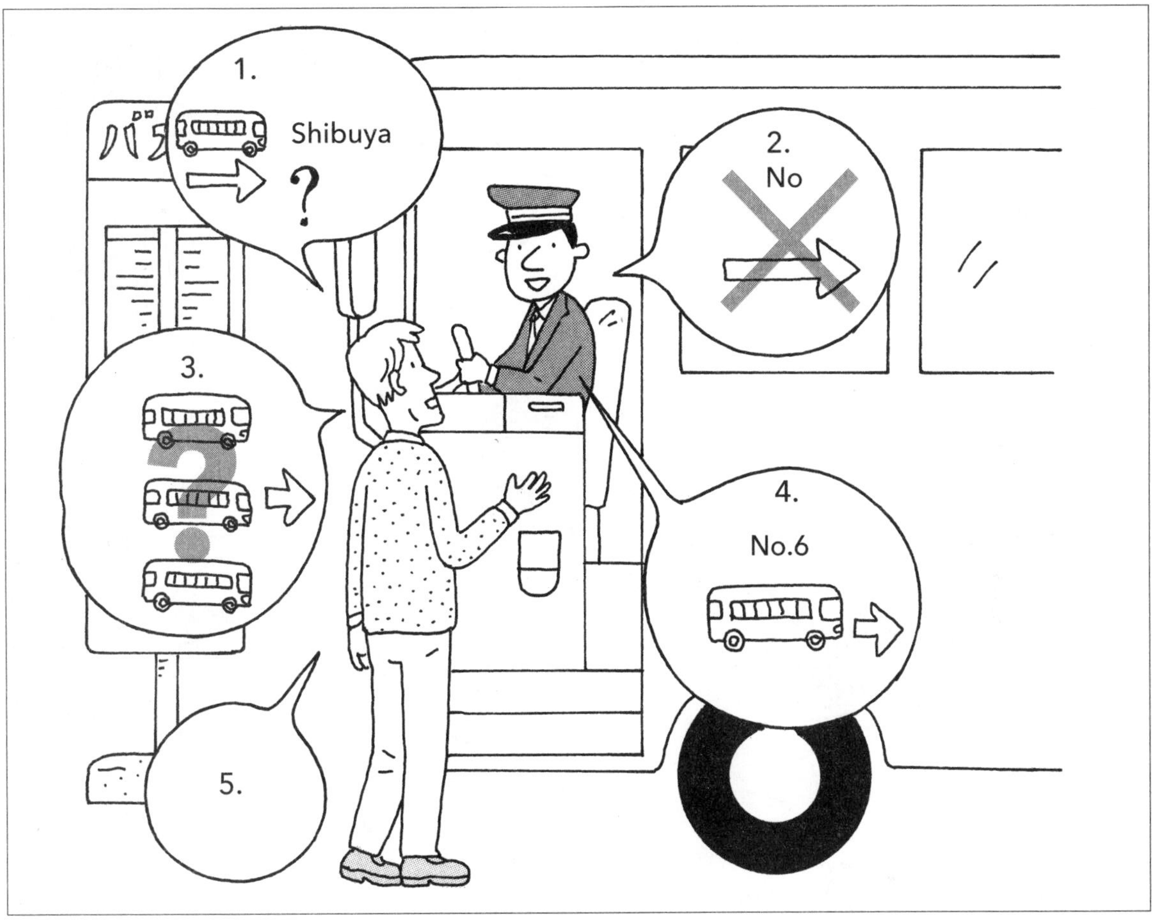

1. Shibuya ?
2. No
3.
4. No.6
5.

Sumisu: [1] Sumimasen. Kono basu wa <u>Shibuya</u> ni ikimasu ka.
Basu no untenshu: [2] Iie, ikimasen.
Sumisu: [3] Dono basu ga ikimasu ka.
Basu no untenshu: [4] <u>6-ban no basu</u> ga ikimasu.
Sumisu: [5] Arigatō gozaimasu.

①

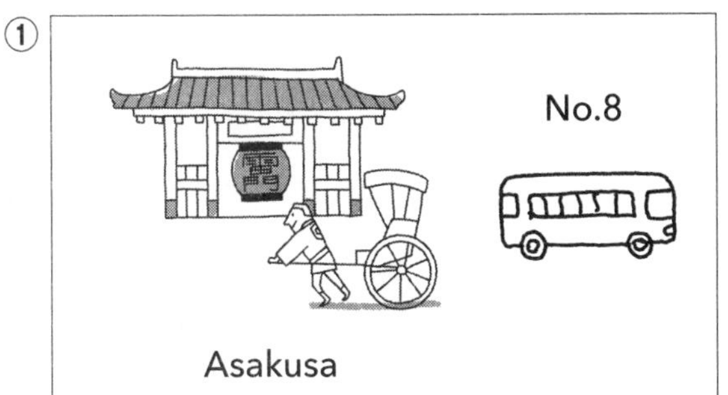

②

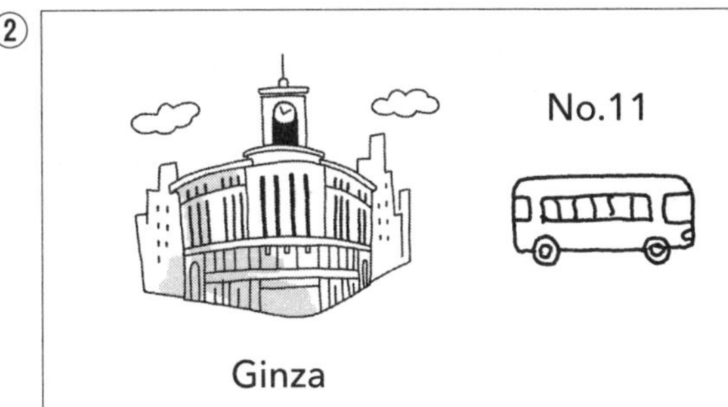

VOCABULARY

Asakusa	Asakusa (tourist spot in Tokyo)

TARGET DIALOGUE

038, 039

Listen to the audio while looking at the illustrations and complete the dialogue.
Smith calls Chan at the Osaka branch office at her mobile number.

1. Chan
2. Tokyo branch Smith
3. Good morning.
4. Good morning.
5. tomorrow Osaka branch
6. from right ?
7. Yes.
8. ? alone Osaka branch
9. No. Kato-san Osaka branch
10.
11. tomorrow
12. Good-bye.
13.

Chan: [1] **Hai, Chan desu.**
Sumisu: [2] ( )
[3] ( )
Chan: [4] **Ohayō gozaimasu.**
Sumisu: [5] ( )
[6] ( )
Chan: [7] **Hai, 1-ji kara desu.** [8] **Hitori de kimasu ka.**
Sumisu: [9] ( )
Chan: [10] **Sō desu ka.** [11] **Dewa ashita.**
Sumisu: [12] ( )
Chan: [13] **Shitsureishimasu.**

Going Places (2): I'm Going by Shinkansen

PRACTICE ①

Make up dialogues following the patterns of the examples and based on the information provided.

A and B are talking about B's schedule for next month.

September

sun	mon	tue	wed	thu	fri	sat
1	2 2. e.g.	3 summer vacation	4	5	6 trip to Kyoto	7
8	9	10 business trip	11	12	13	14 party
15 1. e.g. festival	16	17	18	19	20	21
22	23	24 Nakamura's birthday	25	26	27	28
29	30 meeting					

1. e.g. **A: O-matsuri wa itsu desu ka.**
B: 9-gatsu 15-nichi desu.

2. e.g. **A: Natsu-yasumi wa itsu kara itsu made desu ka.**
B: Raigetsu no futsuka kara nanoka made desu.

PRACTICE ②

Make up dialogues following the pattern of the example and based on the information provided.

e.g. ① ② ③ ④ ⑤

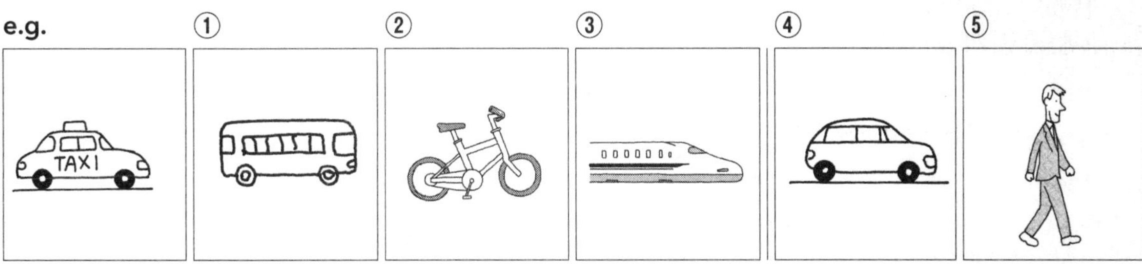

e.g. **A: Nan de ikimasu ka.**
B: Takushī de ikimasu.

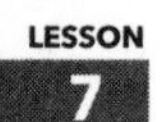

PRACTICE ③

Read the following passage and answer the questions below.

Ema-san wa senshū no do-yōbi ni Nakamura-san to basu de Sasaki-san no uchi ni ikimashita. Ema-san wa takushī de uchi ni kaerimashita. Nakamura-san wa chikatetsu de uchi ni kaerimashita.

① Ema-san wa itsu Sasaki-san no uchi ni ikimashita ka.

② Ema-san wa dare to Sasaki-san no uchi ni ikimashita ka.

③ Nakamura-san wa nan de uchi ni kaerimashita ka.

PRACTICE ④

040

Listen to the audio while looking at the illustrations. Then practice by substituting the underlined words with words shown in the illustrations below.

Emma and someone from the Kyoto branch office are speaking on the phone.

Kyōto-shisha no hito: [1] **Raishū no getsu-yōbi ni sochira ni ikimasu.**
Ema: [2] **Nan-ji ni kimasu ka.**
Kyōto-shisha no hito: [3] **<u>9-ji</u> ni ikimasu.**
Ema: [4] **Nan de kimasu ka.**
Kyōto-shisha no hito: [5] **<u>Shinkansen</u> de ikimasu.**
Ema: [6] **Sō desu ka.**

①

②
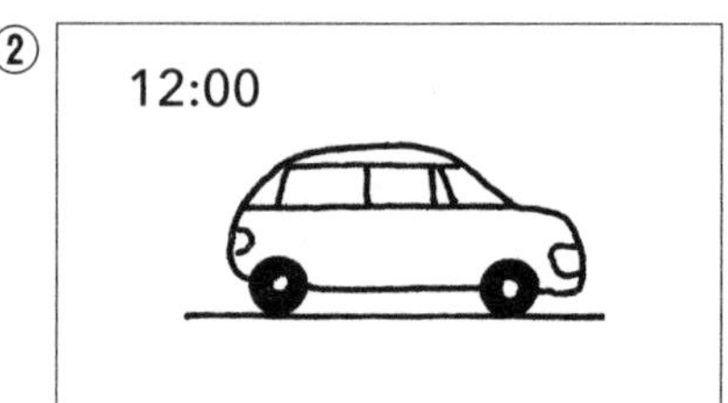

SPEAKING PRACTICE ①

041, 042

Listen to the audio while looking at the illustrations and complete the dialogue.

Kato and Smith arrive at the Osaka branch office and Chan shows them to the meeting room.

Chan: [1] **Dōzo.**

Katō: [2] **(** **)**

Sumisu: [3] **(** **)**

Chan: [4] **Dōzo okake kudasai.**

Sumisu: [5] **Arigatō gozaimasu.**

SPEAKING PRACTICE ②

Listen to the audio while looking at the illustration. Then practice by substituting the underlined words with words shown in the illustration below.

Nakamura and Raja are talking during their break.

e.g.
1.
2. last year Sept.
3. summer vacation India
4. No.
5.

Nakamura: [1] **Raja-san wa itsu Nihon ni kimashita ka.**
Raja: [2] **Kyonen no 9-gatsu ni kimashita.**
Nakamura: [3] **Sō desu ka. Natsu-yasumi ni Indo ni kaerimasu ka.**
Raja: [4] **Iie, kaerimasen.**
[5] **Tomodachi to Hokkaidō ni ikimasu.**

①

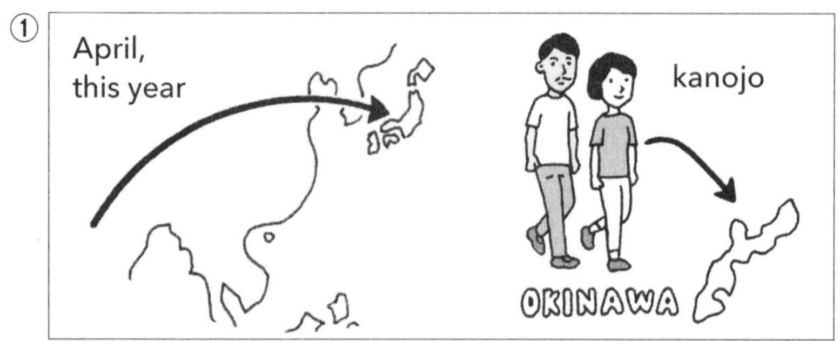

VOCABULARY

kanojo	girlfriend, she

SPEAKING PRACTICE ③

 044

Listen to the audio while looking at the illustrations. Then practice by substituting the underlined words with words shown in the illustrations below.

Smith and Emma are working.

1. meeting

2. 8th next month

3. 4th 8th ?

4. 8th

5. 8th, right

Sumisu: [1] **Kaigi wa itsu desu ka.**
Ema: [2] **Raigetsu no yōka desu.**
Sumisu: [3] **E? Yokka desu ka, yōka desu ka.**
Ema: [4] **Yōka desu.**
Sumisu: [5] **Yōka desu ne.**

①
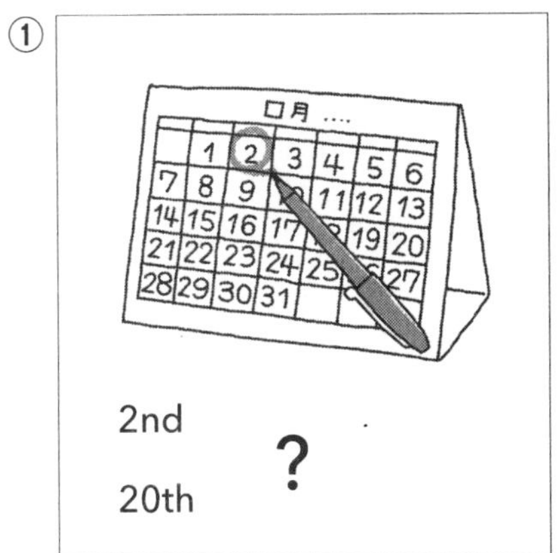

②
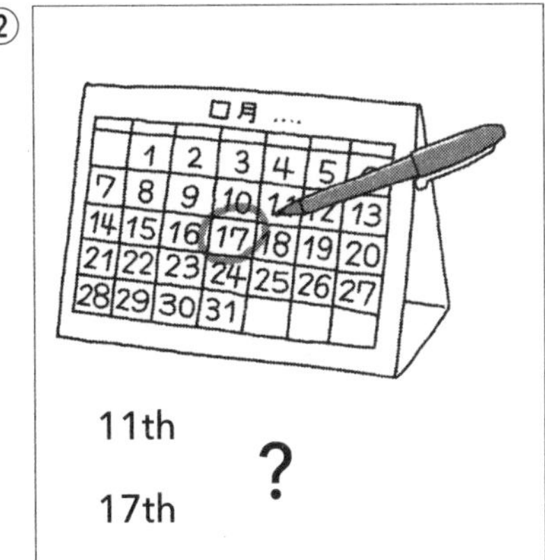

TARGET DIALOGUE

045, 046

Listen to the audio while looking at the illustration and complete the dialogue.

Smith is carrying a suitcase. Nakamura notices and calls out to him.

Nakamura: [1] **A, Sumisu-san, (**   **)**
Sumisu: [2] **Ee, Katō-san to Ōsaka-shisha ni ikimasu. Kin-yōbi ni Tōkyō ni kaerimasu.**
Nakamura: [3] **(**   **)**
Sumisu: [4] **Iie, shinkansen de ikimasu.**
Nakamura: [5] **(**   **) Itterasshai.**

LESSON 8 Doing Things (1): I'm Going to Eat Tempura

PRACTICE ①

Make up sentences or dialogues following the patterns of the examples and based on the information provided.

1. & 2. e.g.

①

②

③

④

⑤

⑥

⑦

⑧

⑨

1. e.g. Sumisu-san wa sutēki o tabemasu.

2. e.g. A: Sumisu-san wa nani o tabemasu ka.
   B: Sutēki o tabemasu.

PRACTICE ②

Make up dialogues following the pattern of the example and based on the information provided.

e.g.

①

②

e.g. A: Sumisu-san wa nani o tabemashita ka.
B: Nani mo tabemasendeshita.

PRACTICE ③

Make up sentences or dialogues following the patterns of the examples and based on the information provided.

1. e.g. Sumisu-san wa resutoran de ban-gohan o tabemasu.

2. e.g. A: Sumisu-san wa doko de ban-gohan o tabemasu ka.
   B: Resutoran de tabemasu.

3. e.g. Sumisu-san wa kinō kōen de tenisu o shimashita.

4. e.g. A: Sumisu-san wa doko de tenisu o shimashita ka.
   B: Kōen de shimashita.

5. e.g. A: Sumisu-san wa itsu tenisu o shimashita ka.
   B: Kinō shimashita.

VOCABULARY

kafe	café
Nihongo no gakkō	Japanese-language school

PRACTICE ④

047

Listen to the audio while looking at the illustrations. Then practice by substituting the underlined words with words shown in the illustrations below.

Suzuki and Chan are talking during their break.

Suzuki: [1] **Shūmatsu ni nani o shimashita ka.**
Chan: [2] **Nakamura-san to shokuji o shimashita.**
Suzuki: [3] **Doko de shimashita ka.**
Chan: [4] **Ginza de shimashita.**
Suzuki: [5] **Sō desu ka.**

①

②

VOCABULARY

shokuji o shimasu	have a meal

SPEAKING PRACTICE ①

048, 049

Make up a dialogue looking at the illustrations. Then listen to the audio and check yourself.
Suzuki phones a tempura restaurant called "Tenmasa."

TENMASA
1.
2.
reservation
3.
Thank you.
5.
How many?
4.
Sat. 7:00
7.
Yes.
name
and
8.
XXXX-XXXX
6.

Mise no hito: [1]Tenmasa de gozaimasu.
Suzuki: [2]( )
Mise no hito: [3]Hai, arigatō gozaimasu.
Suzuki: [4]( )
Mise no hito: [5]Nan-mei sama desu ka.
Suzuki : [6]( )
Mise no hito: [7]Hai, wakarimashita.
[8]Dewa, o-namae to o-denwa-bangō o onegaishimasu.

SPEAKING PRACTICE ②

050, 051

Make up a dialogue looking at the illustrations. Then listen to the audio and check yourself.
On Monday morning, Nakamura is talking to Smith.

Nakamura: [1] **Kinō nani o shimashita ka.**
Sumisu: [2] ( )
Nakamura: [3] **Nani o kaimashita ka.**
Sumisu: [4] ( )

TARGET DIALOGUE

 052, 053

Listen to the audio while looking at the illustrations and complete the dialogue.
Smith and Sasaki are talking during their break.

Sasaki: [1] Shūmatsu ni nani o shimasu ka.

Sumisu: [2] ( )

Sasaki: [3] Sō desu ka. Ii desu ne.

Sumisu: [4] ( )

Sasaki: [5] Nichi-yōbi ni tomodachi to kabuki o mimasu.

Sumisu: [6] ( )

PRACTICE ①

Fill in the blanks with the appropriate words.

① Tanaka-san no ____________

② Tanaka-san no ____________

③ Tanaka-san no ____________

④ Tanaka-san no ____________

⑤ ____________

⑥ ____________

⑦ ____________

⑧ ____________

⑨ Sasaki-san no ____________

⑩ ____________

PRACTICE ②

Make up dialogues following the pattern of the example and based on the information provided.

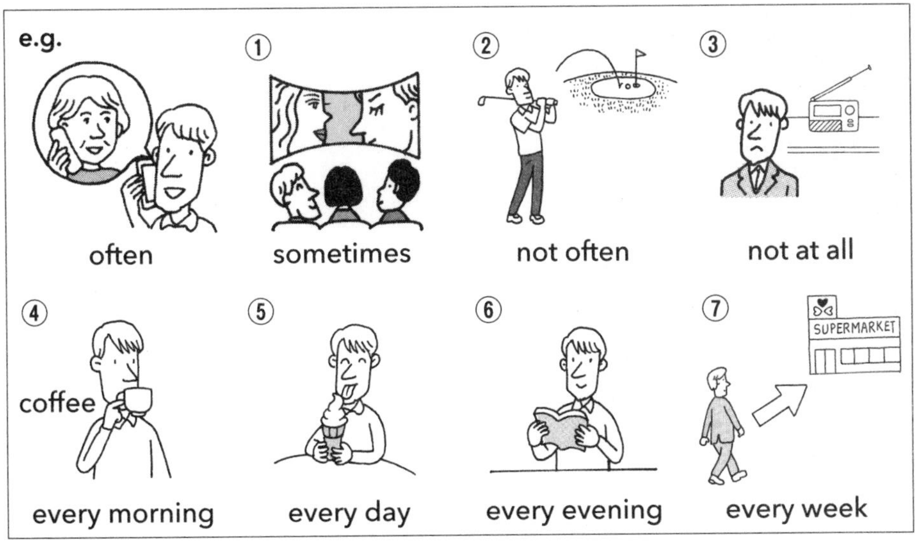

e.g. Suzuki: Sumisu-san wa yoku okāsan ni denwa o shimasu ka.
Sumisu: Hai, yoku shimasu.

PRACTICE ③

Read the following sentences and answer the questions below.

Suzuki-san wa do-yōbi ni pātī de Harisu-san ni aimashita.

Suzuki-san wa Harisu-san ni mēru-adoresu o kikimashita.

Harisu-san wa Suzuki-san ni mēru-adoresu o oshiemashita.

Suzuki-san wa nichi-yōbi ni Harisu-san ni mēru o okurimashita.

1. **Suzuki-san wa pātī de dare ni aimashita ka.**

2. **Suzuki-san wa Harisu-san ni nani o kikimashita ka.**

3. **Harisu-san wa Suzuki-san ni nani o oshiemashita ka.**

4. **Suzuki-san wa nichi-yōbi ni nani o shimashita ka.**

PRACTICE ④

054

Make up a dialogue looking at the illustration. Then listen to the audio and check yourself. Practice by substituting the underlined words with words shown in the illustrations below.

Suzuki and Smith are talking during their break.

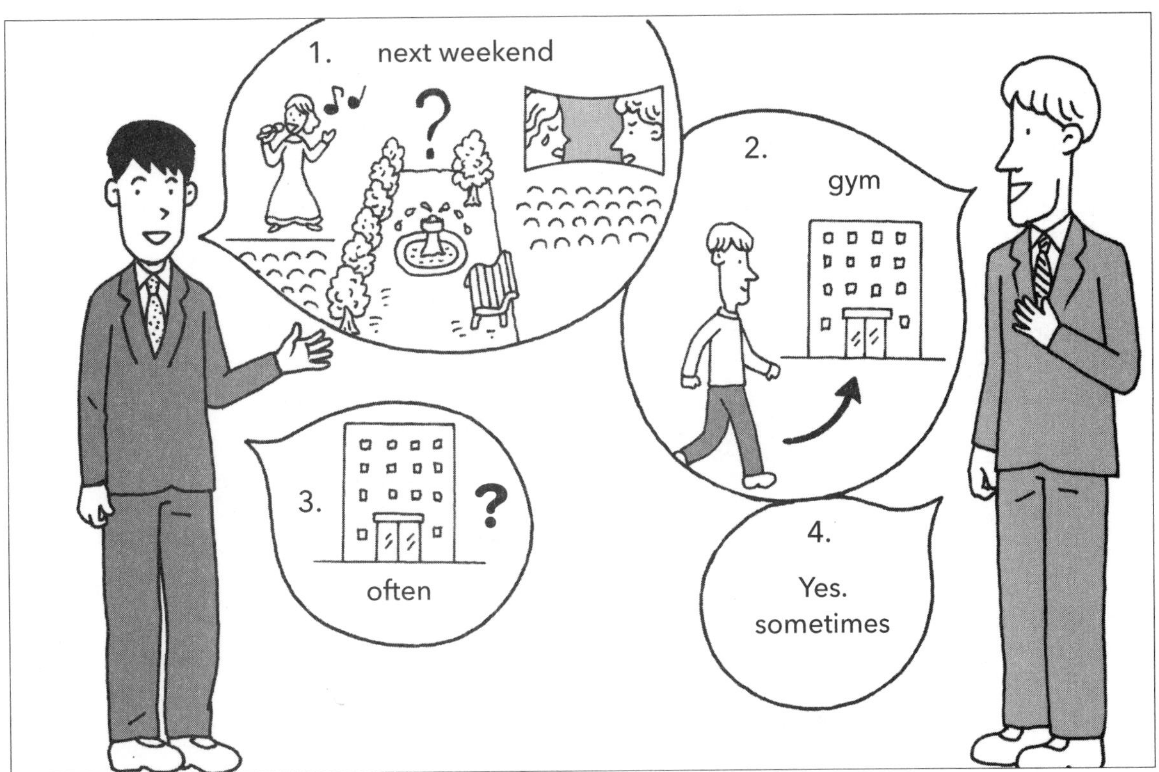

Suzuki: [1] **Kondo no shūmatsu ni nani o shimasu ka.**
Sumisu: [2] **Jimu ni ikimasu.**
Suzuki: [3] **Sumisu-san wa yoku jimu ni ikimasu ka.**
Sumisu: [4] **Hai, tokidoki ikimasu.**

① 

② 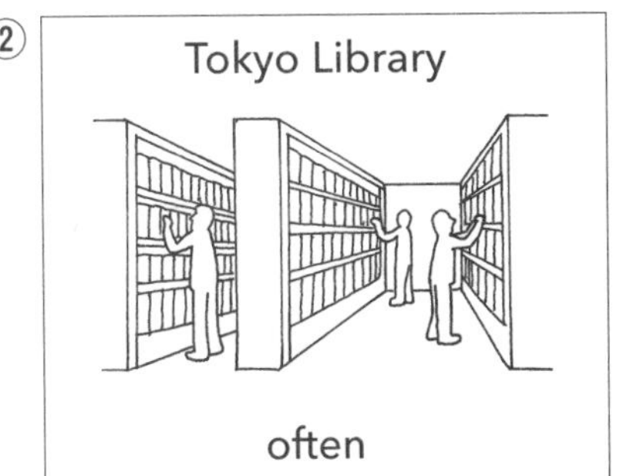

SPEAKING PRACTICE ①

Listen to the audio while looking at the illustrations and complete the dialogue.

Suzuki is in a restaurant with a friend and is about to order.

1. What do you recommend ?

2. How about this?

3. x 2

4. ?

5.

6.

Suzuki: [1]( )

Mise no hito: [2]Kochira desu.

Suzuki: [3]( )

Mise no hito: [4]Hai. O-nomimono wa?

Suzuki: [5]( )

Mise no hito: [6]Hai.

SPEAKING PRACTICE ②

057

Listen to the audio while looking at the illustration. Then practice by substituting the underlined words with words shown in the box below.

Having finished their meal, they call the restaurant employee.

Suzuki: [1] **Sumimasen. O-kaikei o onegaishimasu.**
Mise no hito: [2] **Hai.**
Suzuki: [3] **Betsubetsu ni onegaishimasu.**
Mise no hito: [4] **Hai.**

① issho ni

VOCABULARY

issho ni	together, with

TARGET DIALOGUE

058, 059

Listen to the audio while looking at the illustrations and complete the dialogue.
Smith and Suzuki have arrived at a tempura restaurant in Ginza.

1.
2. Suzuki
3.
4. nice
5. often ?
6. Yes, sometimes
7. last week
8. Really?
9.

Mise no hito: [1] Irasshaimase.
Suzuki: [2] ( )
Mise no hito: [3] Suzuki-sama desu ne. Dōzo kochira e.
Sumisu: [4] Ii mise desu ne.
[5] Suzuki-san wa yoku kono mise ni kimasu ka.
Suzuki: [6] ( )
[7] ( )
Sumisu: [8] E, hontō desu ka.
Sumisu and Suzuki: [9] A, Gurīn-san!

Describe Smith's life in Tokyo.

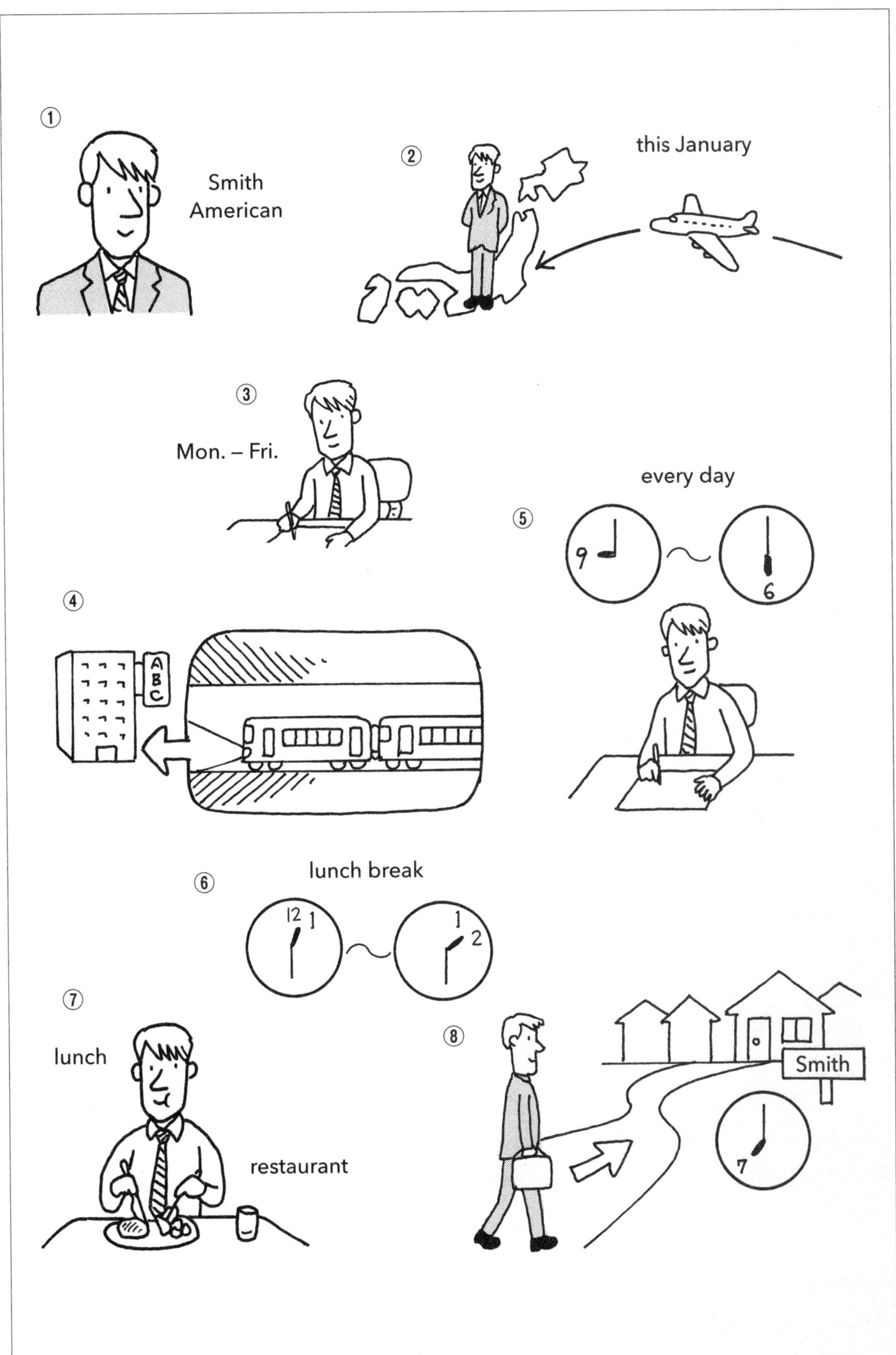

LESSON **10** # Describing Things: It's Delicious

PRACTICE ①

Fill in the blanks in the chart with the appropriate words.

	As predicate: Present form		Modifying noun
	aff.	*neg.*	
big	ōkii desu	ōkikunai desu	ōkii
new, fresh	①	②	③
good, nice	④	⑤	⑥
bad	⑦	⑧	⑨
hot	⑩	⑪	⑫
delicious	⑬	⑭	⑮
quiet	shizuka desu	shizuka ja arimasen	shizukana
convenient	⑯	⑰	⑱
pretty, clean	⑲	⑳	㉑

PRACTICE ②

Make up sentences following the pattern of the example and based on the information provided.

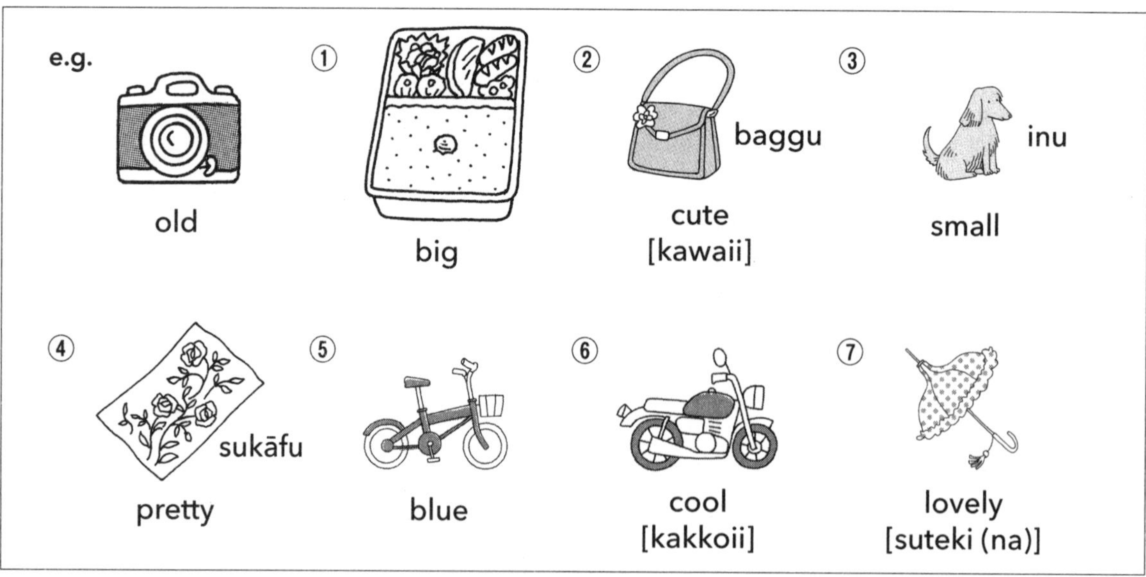

e.g. Sono <u>furui kamera</u> wa Ema-san no desu.

VOCABULARY

baggu	handbag	**inu**	dog	**kakkoii**	cool, looks good, smart looking
kawaii	cute, pretty	**sukāfu**	scarf	**suteki (na)**	lovely

PRACTICE ③

060

Listen to the audio while looking at the illustration. Then practice by substituting the words shown in the illustrations below.

In the morning, Chan and Sasaki are engaging in small talk.

Chan: [1]Kyō wa samui desu ne.
Sasaki: [2]Ee, hontō ni samui desu ne.

①

②

good weather

③

warm

④

cool

SPEAKING PRACTICE ①

061, 062

Listen to the audio while looking at the illustrations and complete the dialogue.
Emma visits the Sasakis' home. She rings the doorbell.

Sasaki: [1] Hai, donata desu ka.
Ema: [2] Ema desu.
Sasaki: [3] A, chotto matte kudasai.
[4] Dōzo.
Ema: [5] (   )

SPEAKING PRACTICE ②

063, 064

Listen to the audio while looking at the illustrations and complete the dialogue.

Smith is looking at rice bowls in an antique shop.

Sumisu: [1] Kore wa ikura desu ka.

Mise no hito: [2] 8,000-en desu.

Sumisu: [3] (   )

Mise no hito: [4] Kochira wa 6,500-en desu.

Sumisu: [5] Ja, sore o kudasai.

TARGET DIALOGUE

065, 066

Listen to the audio while looking at the illustrations and complete the dialogue.
Emma is visiting the Sasakis' home. She is enjoying their hospitality.

1.
2. Thank you.
3.
4. Yes.
5.
6. ?
7. Yes. Kyoto
8.

Sasaki: [1] **O-cha o dōzo.**

Ema: [2] ( )

Sasaki: [3] **O-kashi wa ikaga desu ka.**

Ema: [4] ( )

[5] ( )

[6] ( )

Sasaki: [7] **Ee, sō desu. Kyōto no o-kashi desu.**

Ema: [8] ( )

LESSON 11 Describing Impressions: It Was Beautiful

PRACTICE ①

Make up a dialogue looking at the illustration. Then practice by substituting the underlined words with words shown in the illustrations below.

e.g. **Nakamura:** [1] **Kinō no pātī wa tanoshikatta desu ka.**
Ema: [2] **Hai, tanoshikatta desu.**
Sumisu: [3] **Iie, tanoshikunakatta desu.**

① 

② 

PRACTICE ②

Make up sentences following the pattern of the example and based on the information provided.

e.g.

①

②

③

e.g. Senshū wa isogashikatta desu ga, konshū wa hima desu.

PRACTICE ③

Listen to the audio while looking at the illustrations. Then practice by substituting the underlined words with words shown in the illustrations below.

Nakamura and Smith are talking during their break.

1. weekend ?

2. Hokkaido

3. how ?

4. very fun

Nakamura: [1] **Sumisu-san, shūmatsu ni nani o shimashita ka.**
Sumisu: [2] **Hokkaidō de sukī o shimashita.**
Nakamura: [3] **Dō deshita ka.**
Sumisu: [4] **Totemo tanoshikatta desu.**

①
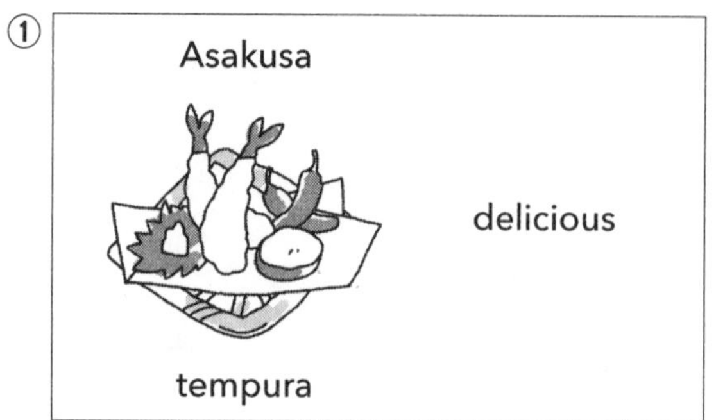

②
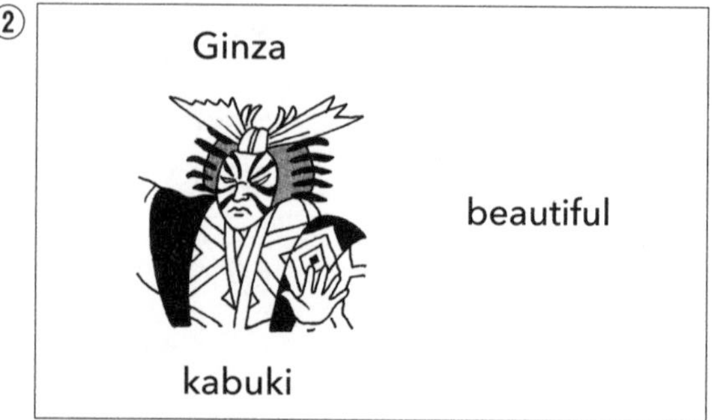

SPEAKING PRACTICE ①

068, 069

Listen to the audio while looking at the illustrations and complete the dialogue.
Emma is visiting the Sasakis' home.

Ema: 1 ( )
2 ( )
Sasaki: 3 **Dō itashimashite.**
Ema: 4 ( )
Sasaki: 5 **Watashitachi mo tanoshikatta desu.**
6 **Mata kite kudasai.**

SPEAKING PRACTICE ②

070

Listen to the audio while looking at the illustrations. Then practice by substituting the underlined words with words shown in the illustrations below.

On Monday morning, Smith and Nakamura are talking at the office.

e.g.

Hakone
1.
last weekend

Hakone
2.
3.
4.
Thank you.

6.
5.
Hakone
how ?

Sumisu:	1 Shūmatsu ni Hakone ni ikimashita.
	2 Kore, Hakone no o-miyage desu.
	3 Dōzo.
Nakamura:	4 Arigatō gozaimasu.
	5 Hakone wa dō deshita ka.
Sumisu:	6 Totemo yokatta desu.

①
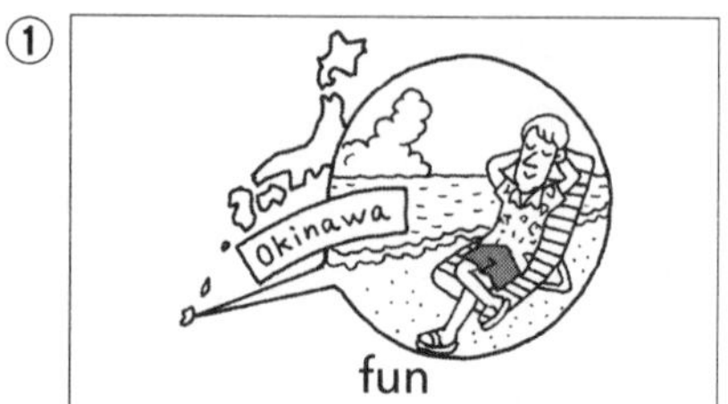

②

SPEAKING PRACTICE ③

071, 072

Listen to the audio while looking at the illustration and complete the dialogue.
Nakamura received a souvenir from Smith yesterday.

Nakamura: [1]( )
[2]( )

Sumisu: [3]Sō desu ka.
[4]Yokatta desu.

TARGET DIALOGUE

073, 074

Listen to the audio while looking at the illustrations and complete the dialogue.
At the Sasakis' house, Emma is talking with the Sasakis.

1. Mt. Fuji
2. How ?
3.
4. photo?
5.
6.
7. How long?
8. about 8 hours
9. hard, but fun

Ema: [1]( )
Sasaki: [2]Dō deshita ka.
Ema: [3]( )
Sasaki: [4]Shashin o torimashita ka.
Ema: [5]( )
Sasaki: [6]Hontō ni kirei desu ne.
[7]Donokurai arukimashita ka.
Ema: [8]( )
[9]( )

LESSON 12 Asking about Places: What Is at Nikko?

PRACTICE ①

Make up sentences or dialogues following the patterns of the examples and based on the information provided.

1. e.g. 1-kai ni konbini ga arimasu.

2. e.g. A: 1-kai ni nani ga arimasu ka.
B: Konbini ga arimasu.

PRACTICE ②

Make up sentences or dialogues following the patterns of the examples and based on the information provided.

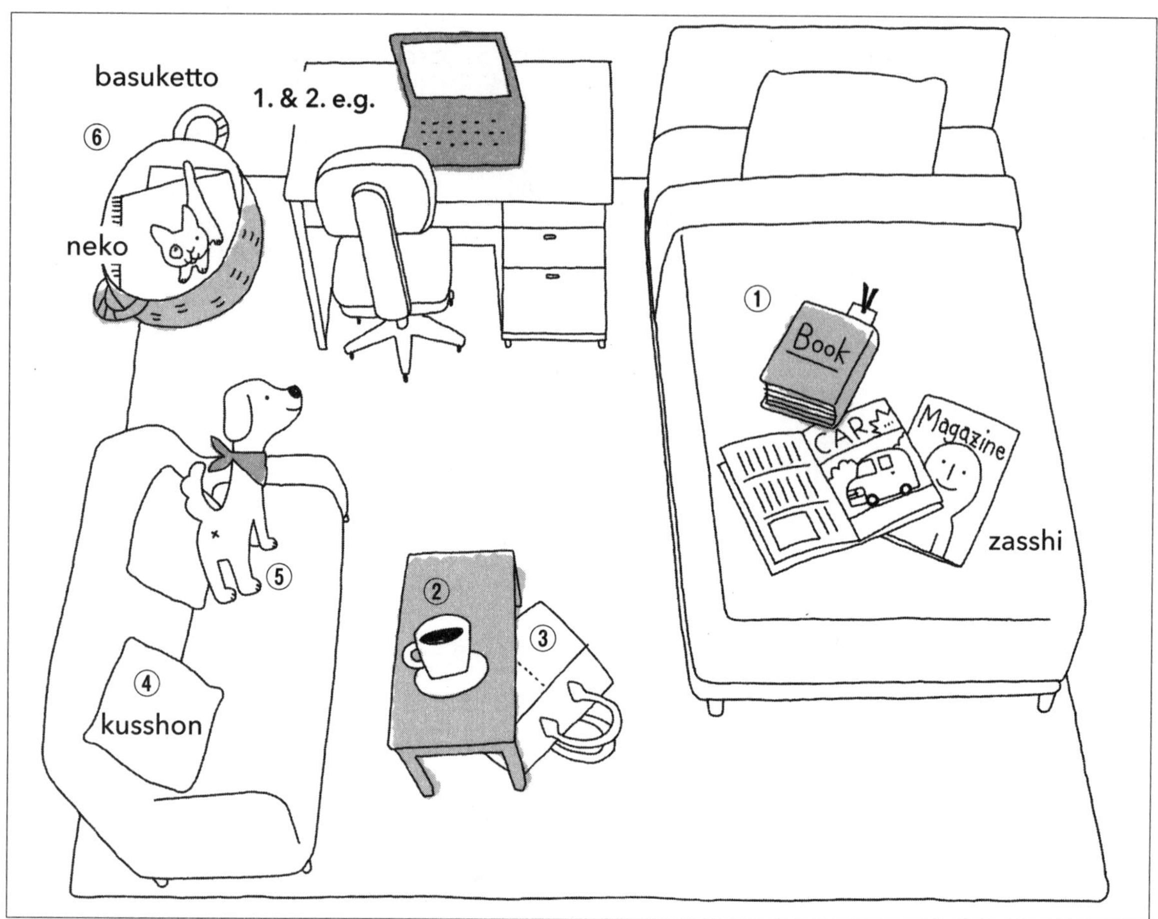

1. e.g. **Tsukue no ue ni pasokon ga arimasu.**

2. e.g. **A: Tsukue no ue ni nani ga arimasu ka.**
B: Pasokon ga arimasu.

VOCABULARY

zasshi	magazine	**basuketto**	basket
kusshon	cushion	**neko**	cat

PRACTICE ③

075

Listen to the audio while looking at the illustrations. Then practice by substituting the underlined words with words shown in the illustrations below.

Nakamura and Smith are talking during their break.

1. Sun. Kamakura

2. Is that so?

3. Kamakura

4. Shrines and temples etc.

5. Good!

Nakamura: [1] **Nichi-yōbi ni kuruma de Kamakura ni ikimasu.**

Sumisu: [2] **Sō desu ka.**

[3] **Kamakura ni nani ga arimasu ka.**

Nakamura: [4] **Jinja ya o-tera ga arimasu.**

Sumisu: [5] **Ii desu ne.**

①

②

SPEAKING PRACTICE

076, 077

Listen to the audio while looking at the illustrations and complete the dialogue.
Nakamura and Raja are talking during their break.

Nakamura: [1] Raja-san no uchi wa Indo no doko desu ka.
Raja: [2] Goa desu.
Nakamura: [3] Donna tokoro desu ka.
Raja: [4] ( )
[5] ( )
Nakamura: [6] Nani ga yūmei desu ka.
Raja: [7] ( )

TARGET DIALOGUE

078, 079

Listen to the audio while looking at the illustrations and complete the dialogue.

Nakamura and Raja are talking during their break.

1. Nikko Sat.
2. ? Nikko
3. etc.
4. onsen, too
5. onsen ?
6. this, Japanese spas
7. good!

Nakamura: [1] Do-yōbi ni Ema-san to Nikkō ni ikimasu.

Raja: [2] ( )

Nakamura: [3] Ōkii o-tera ya jinja ga arimasu.

[4] Onsen mo arimasu.

Raja: [5] ( )

Nakamura: [6] Kore desu. Nihon no supa desu yo.

Raja: [7] ( )

PRACTICE ①

Make up sentences or dialogues following the patterns of the examples and based on the information provided.

e.g.1

Ribingu ni sofā ga futatsu arimasu.

e.g.2

Niwa ni onna no hito ga futari imasu.

e.g.3

A: Ribingu ni sofā ga ikutsu arimasu ka.

B: Futatsu arimasu.

e.g.4

A: Niwa ni onna no hito ga nan-nin imasu ka.

B: Futari imasu.

VOCABULARY

ribingu	living room	**piza**	pizza	**niwa**	garden, lawn
kitchin	kitchen	**supūn**	spoon		

PRACTICE ②

Make up dialogues following the patterns of the examples and based on the information provided.

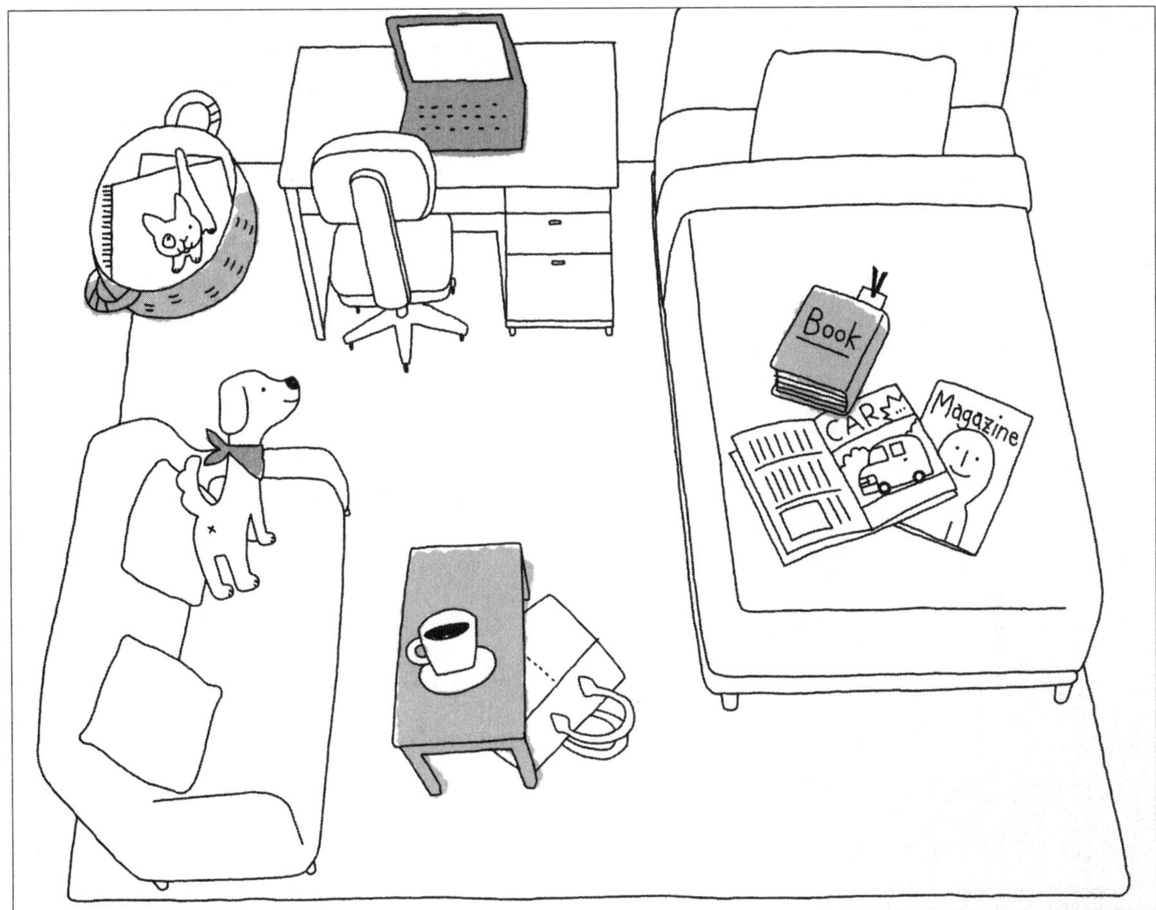

e.g.1

A: Hon wa doko ni arimasu ka.

B: Beddo no ue ni arimasu.

e.g.2

A: Neko wa doko ni imasu ka.

B: Basuketto no naka ni imasu.

PRACTICE ③

Listen to the audio while looking at the illustration. Then practice by substituting the underlined words with the words shown in the illustrations below.

Emma is asking the hotel concierge a question.

1.
HOTEL
near?
2.
No.
a bit far
3. about 15 min.
4.
5.
Thank you.

Ema: [1] Taki wa koko kara chikai desu ka.
Hoteru no hito: [2] Iie, chotto tōi desu.
[3] Basu de 15-fun gurai desu.
Ema: [4] Sō desu ka.
[5] Dōmo arigatō gozaimasu.

①

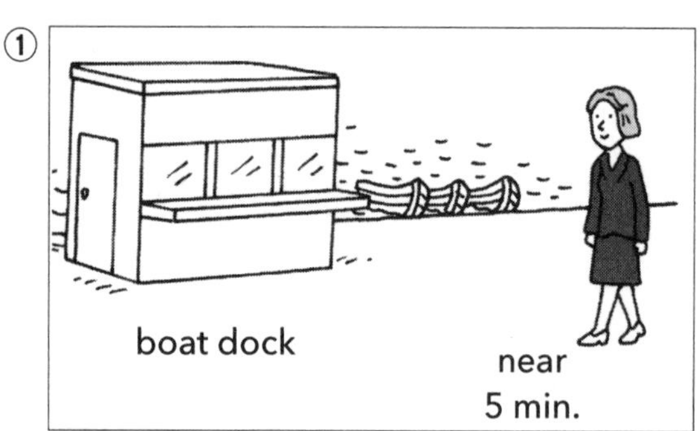

②

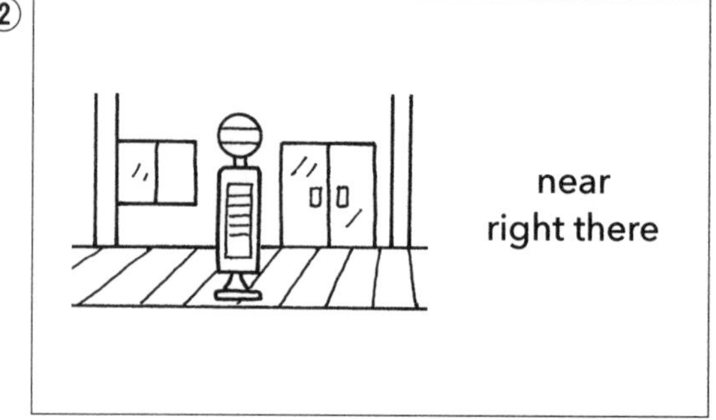

SPEAKING PRACTICE ①

081, 082

Listen to the audio while looking at the illustration and complete the dialogue.

Kato and Emma are working.

Katō: [1]( )

Ema: [2]Koko ni arimasu. [3]Dōzo.

SPEAKING PRACTICE ②

083

Listen to the audio while looking at the illustration. Then practice by substituting the underlined words with words shown in the illustrations below.

Kato telephones Suzuki, who is out of the office.

Katō: [1]Suzuki-san, ima doko desu ka.

Suzuki: [2]Ima <u>Nozomi Depāto</u> ni imasu.

Katō: [3]Nan-ji goro kaisha ni kaerimasu ka.

Suzuki: [4]<u>3-ji</u> ni kaerimasu.

①

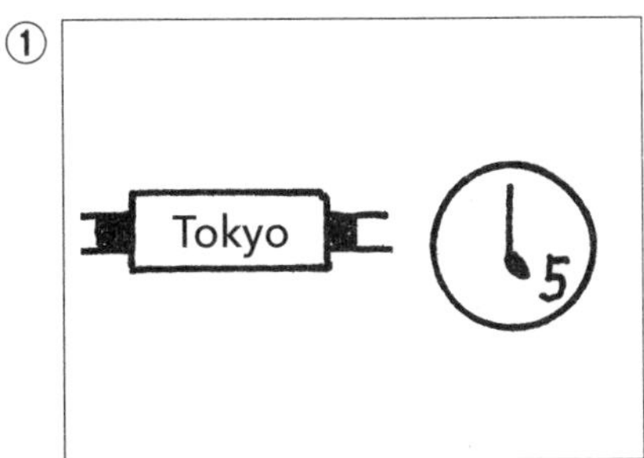

②

TARGET DIALOGUE

 084, 085

Listen to the audio while looking at the illustrations and complete the dialogue.

Nakamura and Emma are in a souvenir shop in Nikko.

Nakamura: [1] (   )

Mise no hito: [2] **Ee, Sobaichi ga oishii desu yo.**

Ema: [3] (   )

Mise no hito: [4] **Asoko ni o-tera ga arimasu ne.** [5] **Sobaichi wa ano o-tera no mae desu.**

Ema: [6] (   )

[7] (   )

Mise no hito: [8] **Iie, chotto tōi desu.** [9] **Basu de 15-fun gurai desu.**

Ema: [10] (   )

[11] (   )

PRACTICE ①

Make up dialogues following the patterns of the examples and based on the information provided.

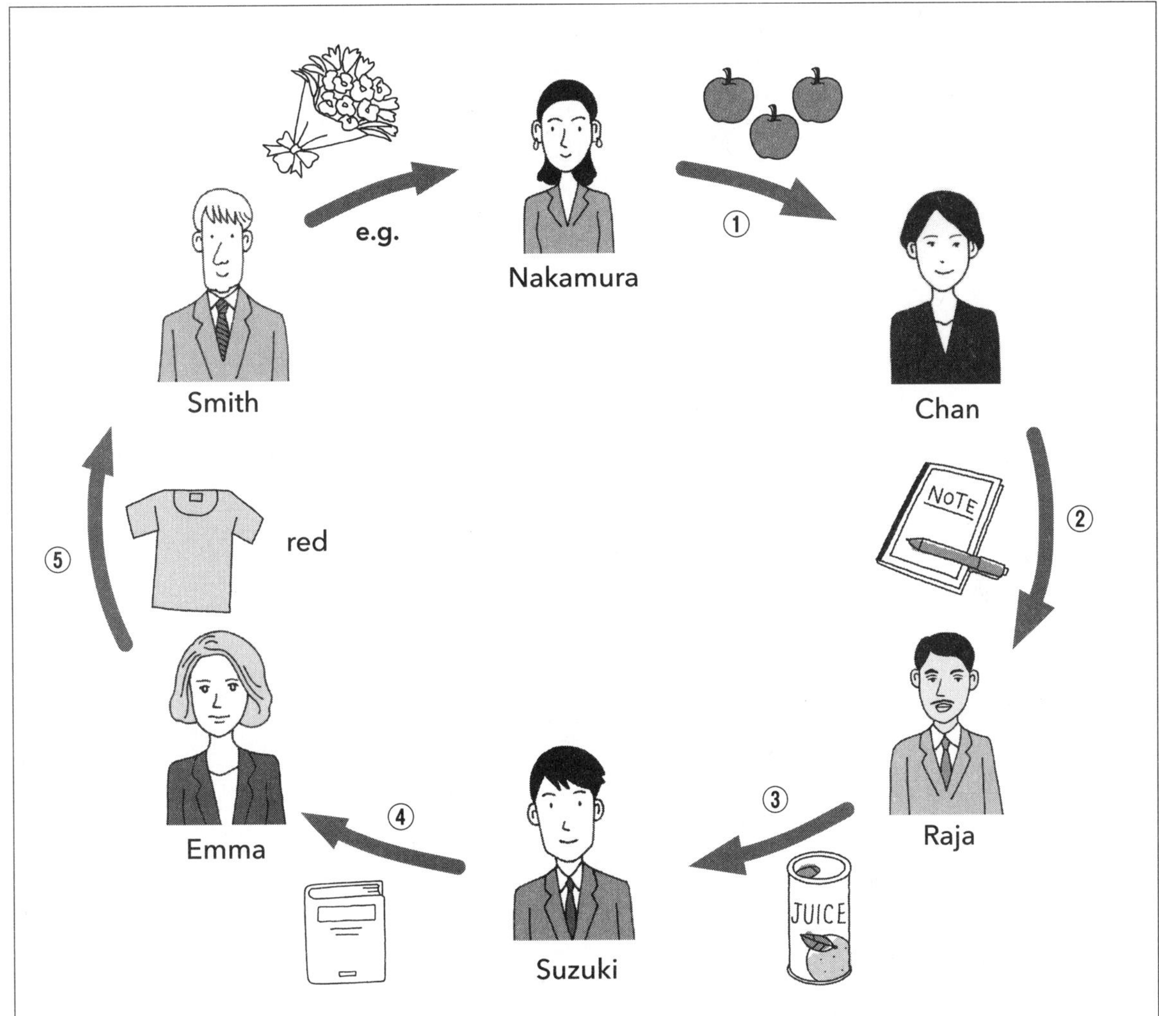

1. e.g. A: Sumisu-san wa Nakamura-san ni nani o agemashita ka.
   B: Hana o agemashita.

2. e.g. A: Nakamura-san wa dare ni hana o moraimashita ka.
   B: Sumisu-san ni moraimashita.

PRACTICE ②

Looking at the illustrations, complete the sentences below.

① **Nakamura-san wa Sumisu-san ni kasa o (　　　　　　　　　　　　).**

Sumisu-san wa Nakamura-san ni kasa o (　　　　　　　　　　　　).

② **Sumisu-san wa Nakamura-san ni kasa o kaeshimashita.**

③ **Sumisu-san wa Nakamura-san ni kukkī o (　　　　　　　　　　　　).**

VOCABULARY

kaeshimasu	return, give back

PRACTICE ③

086

Listen to the audio while looking at the illustrations. Then practice by substituting the underlined words with words shown in the illustrations below.

Nakamura is wearing a new necklace.

1.

2.

friend

3.

It suits you well.

4.

Ema: [1] Kireina nekkuresu desu ne.
Nakamura: [2] Ee, tanjōbi ni tomodachi ni moraimashita.
Ema: [3] Yoku niaimasu ne.
Nakamura: [4] Arigatō gozaimasu.

①

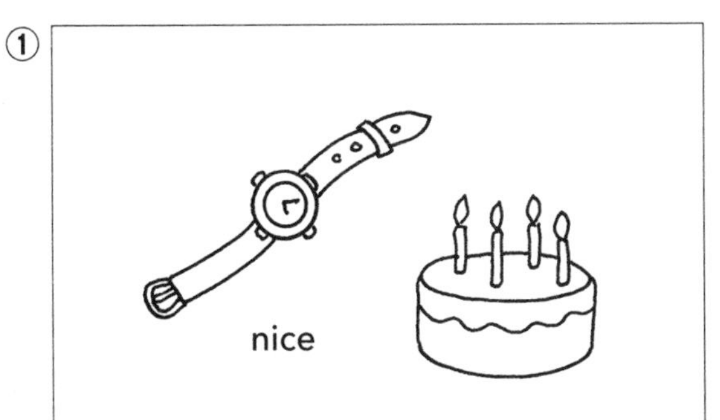

②

SPEAKING PRACTICE

087, 088

Listen to the audio while looking at the illustrations and complete the dialogue.

The train lurches, and Emma steps on the foot of another person standing.

Onna no hito: 1 **Itai!**

Ema: 2 **Sumimasen.**

3 (   )

Onna no hito: 4 **Ee, daijōbu desu.**

Ema: 5 (   )

TARGET DIALOGUE

089, 090

Listen to the audio while looking at the illustrations and complete the dialogue.

Nakamura and Emma are in Nikko. They have gotten off the bus near the waterfall.

Ema: [1] Chotto samui desu ne.

Nakamura: [2] ( )

[3] Kore, dōzo.

Ema: [4] E, ii n desu ka.

Nakamura: [5] ( )

Ema: [6] Arigatō gozaimasu. Sutekina sukāfu desu ne.

Nakamura: [7] ( )

REVIEW 3

Create a dialogue based on the illustrations.

Smith pays a visit to his friend's home.

The two enjoy their visit and then the time comes for Smith to leave.

VOCABULARY

kabin	vase

LESSON 15 Talking about Preferences: I Like Japanese Anime

PRACTICE ①

Fill in the blanks in the chart below with the appropriate word.

	Masu-form	Dictionary form		Masu-form	Dictionary form
go	ikimasu	①	swim	oyogimasu	⑦
sing	utaimasu	②	talk	hanashimasu	⑧
run	hashirimasu	③	eat	tabemasu	⑨
take	torimasu	④	see	mimasu	⑩
drink	nomimasu	⑤	come	kimasu	⑪
draw	kakimasu	⑥	do	shimasu	⑫

PRACTICE ②

Make up sentences following the pattern of the example and based on the information provided.

Smith is introducing someone.

e.g.

①

②

③

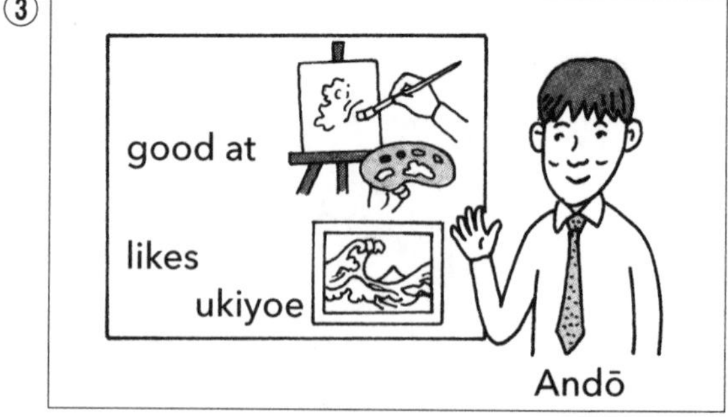

e.g. Sumisu: Kochira wa Aren-san desu.
Aren-san wa ryōri ga jōzu desu. Aka-wain ga suki desu.

VOCABULARY

ryōri	cooking	Honda	Honda (surname)	ukiyoe	ukiyoe (woodblock print)
piano	piano	suiei	swimming	Andō	Ando (surname)

PRACTICE ③

Listen to the audio while looking at the illustrations. Then practice by substituting the underlined words with words shown in the illustrations below.

Nakamura and Smith are talking during their break.

3.
Nakamura-san?

1.

2.
Yes.

4.
me, too

6.

5.
, too.

Nakamura: [1] **Sumisu-san wa ongaku o kiku no ga suki desu ka.**
Sumisu: [2] **Ee, suki desu.**
[3] **Nakamura-san wa?**
Nakamura: [4] **Watashi mo suki desu.**
[5] **Utau no mo suki desu.**
Sumisu: [6] **Sō desu ka. Ii desu ne.**

①

②

VOCABULARY

dōga	video

SPEAKING PRACTICE

092, 093

Listen to the audio while looking at the illustrations and complete the dialogue.
Nakamura and Raja are talking during their break.

Nakamura: [1] Raja-san wa supōtsu ga suki desu ka.
Raja: [2] Hai, suki desu.
Nakamura: [3] Donna supōtsu ga suki desu ka.
Raja: [4] ( )
[5] ( )

TARGET DIALOGUE

094, 095

Listen to the audio while looking at the illustrations and complete the dialogue.

Smith's cousin Paul is visiting Japan.

1. cousin, Paul

2.

3.

4. Japanese anime ♡

5. what kind?

6.

7. Me, too.

8. drawing illustrations too

9. !!!

Sumisu:	[1] **Itoko no Pōru desu.**
Pōru:	[2] **Hajimemashite. Pōru desu.** [3] **Yoroshiku onegaishimasu.**
	[4] **Watashi wa Nihon no anime ga suki desu.**
Suzuki:	[5] ( )
Pōru:	[6] **Robotto no anime ga suki desu.**
Suzuki:	[7] ( )
	[8] ( )
Sumisu and Pōru:	[9] **Wā! Sugoi! Jōzu desu ne!**

Making an Invitation: Shall We Go Together?

PRACTICE ①

Look at the illustration and make up a sentence. Then practice by substituting the underlined words with words shown in the illustrations below.

Nakamura and Emma are talking.

e.g. Nakamura: Ii tenki desu kara, kōen de hiru-gohan o tabemasen ka.

①
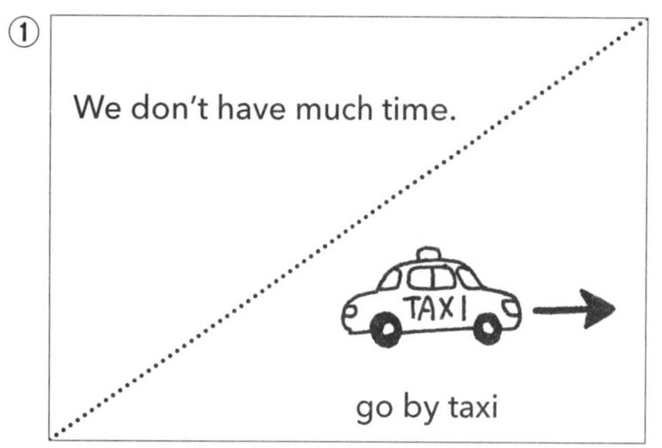

②

③

PRACTICE ②

Look at the illustrations and make up a dialogue. Then practice by substituting the underlined words with words shown in the illustrations below.

Smith and Suzuki are walking together.

e.g.

e.g. Sumisu: [1] Onaka ga sukimashita ne.
Suzuki: [2] Sō desu ne.
Sumisu: [3] Ano resutoran de nanika tabemasen ka.
Suzuki: [4] Ii desu ne. Sō shimashō.

①

②

PRACTICE ③

Listen to the audio while looking at the illustrations. Then practice by substituting the underlined words with words shown in the illustrations below.

Kato invites Smith to the fireworks festival.

Katō: [1] **Do-yōbi ni Asakusa de hanabi-taikai ga arimasu. Issho ni ikimasen ka.**
Sumisu: [2] **Ii desu ne. Zehi.**
[3] **Hanabi-taikai wa nan-ji kara desu ka.**
Katō: [4] **7-ji kara desu.**
[5] **6-ji ni Asakusa Eki no 5-ban deguchi de aimashō.**
Sumisu: [6] **6-ji ni Asakusa Eki no 5-ban deguchi desu ne. Wakarimashita.**

①

②
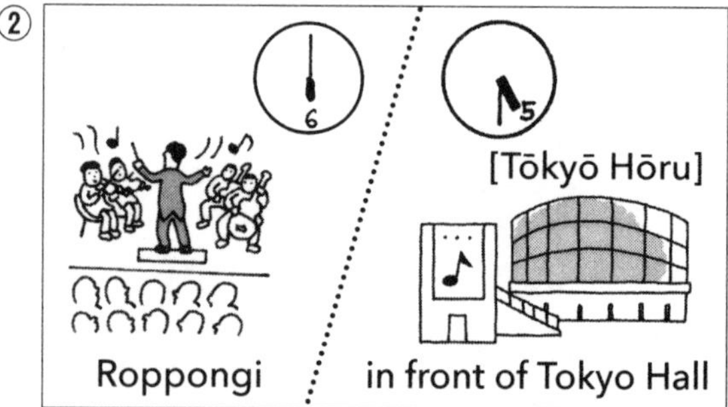

VOCABULARY

5-ban deguchi	Exit No. 5	Tōkyō Hōru	Tokyo Hall (fictitious facility name)

SPEAKING PRACTICE ①

097, 098

Listen to the audio while looking at the illustration and complete the dialogue.

Sasaki is having a party at her home.

Sasaki: [1] Sumisu-san, ( ).

[2] ( )

Sumisu: [3] Arigatō gozaimasu.

[4] Zehi.

SPEAKING PRACTICE ②

Listen to the audio while looking at the illustration. Then practice by substituting the underlined words with words shown in the illustration below.

Nakamura is going to play tennis on Saturday.

1.

2.
together?

3.

4. !

Nakamura: [1] <u>Do-yōbi</u> ni Sumisu-san to <u>tenisu o shimasu.</u>
[2] Ema-san mo issho ni shimasen ka.

Ema: [3] Arigatō gozaimasu.
[4] Zehi.

①

TARGET DIALOGUE

100, 101

Listen to the audio while looking at the illustrations and complete the dialogue.

Suzuki, Paul, and Smith are talking.

1. Akihabara anime event
2. together?
3. !

from
4. ?
from
5.
6. lunch together

7. ?
8.
9.

Suzuki: [1]( )

[2]( )

Pōru: [3]Ii desu ne. Zehi.

[4]Ibento wa nan-ji kara desu ka.

Suzuki: [5]( )

[6]( )

[7]( )

Sumisu: [8]Sumimasen. Anime wa chotto....

Suzuki: [9]Sō desu ka.

CHALLENGE 3

This is the Minato City event calendar. Invite a colleague or friend to an event, and decide at what time and where you will meet.

4-gatsu Minato-shi

Sunday	Monday	Tuesday	Wednesday	Thursday	Friday	Saturday
1	2	3	4	5	6	7
←	**Sakura Matsuri** 10:00 A.M.– 4:00 P.M Nishi Kōen			→	**Yoga Kurasu** 7:15 P.M.– 8:30 P.M. Supōtsu Sentā	**Charitī Bazā** 9:00 A.M.– 4:30 P.M. Higashi Toshokan
8	9	10	11	12	13	14
Charitī Bazā 9:00 A.M.– 4:30 P.M. Higashi Toshokan	**Gorufu Ressun** 6:45 P.M.– 8:00 P.M. Supōtsu Sentā		**Pasokon Seminā** 10:30 A.M.– 12:30 P.M. Minato Sentā		**Yoga Kurasu** 7:15 P.M.– 8:30 P.M. Supōtsu Sentā	**Nihonshu no Ibento** 7:00 P.M.– 9:00 P.M. Minato Resutoran
15	16	17	18	19	20	21
Piano Konsāto 6:30 P.M. Tōkyō Hōru		**Sushi Wākushoppu** 10:00 A.M.– 12:00 P.M. Minato Sentā		**Kōcha Seminā** 1:30 P.M.– 3:30 P.M. Nozomi Depāto	**Yoga Kurasu** 7:15 P.M.– 8:30 P.M. Supōtsu Sentā	**Furī Māketto** 9:00 A.M.– 5:00 P.M. Minami Kōen
22	23	24	25	26	27	28
Furī Māketto 9:00 A.M.– 5:00 P.M. Minami Kōen	**Gorufu Ressun** 6:45 P.M.– 8:00 P.M. Supōtsu Sentā		**Bonsai Wākushoppu** 1:00 P.M.– 3:00 P.M. Minato Sentā		**Yoga Kurasu** 7:15 P.M.– 8:30 P.M. Supōtsu Sentā	**Wain Seminā** 2:00 P.M.– 4:00 P.M. Nozomi Depāto
29	30					

e.g. A : Jūyokka no do-yōbi ni Minato Resutoran de nihonshu no ibento ga arimasu. Issho ni ikimasen ka.
B : Ii desu ne. Zehi. Ibento wa nan-ji kara desu ka.
A : 7-ji kara desu. 6-ji han ni Minato Resutoran no mae de aimashō.
B : Wakarimashita. Tanoshimi desu.
A : Ja, do-yōbi ni.

VOCABULARY

Minato-shi	Minato City (fictitious city name)
shi	city
sakura	cherry tree, cherry blossom
Nishi Kōen	West Park (fictitious park name)
Supōtsu Sentā	Sports Center (fictitious facility name)
charitī-bazā	charity bazaar
Higashi Toshokan	East Library (fictitious library name)
ressun	lesson
seminā	seminar
Minato Sentā	Minato Center (fictitious facility name)
Minato Resutoran	Minato Restaurant (fictitious restaurant name)
wākushoppu	workshop
Minami Kōen	South Park (fictitious park name)
bonsai	bonsai
Tanoshimi desu.	I'm looking forward to it.

PRACTICE ①

Is there something that you always do before engaging in some activity? Taking hints from the example, make up sentences expressing a sequence of two activities.

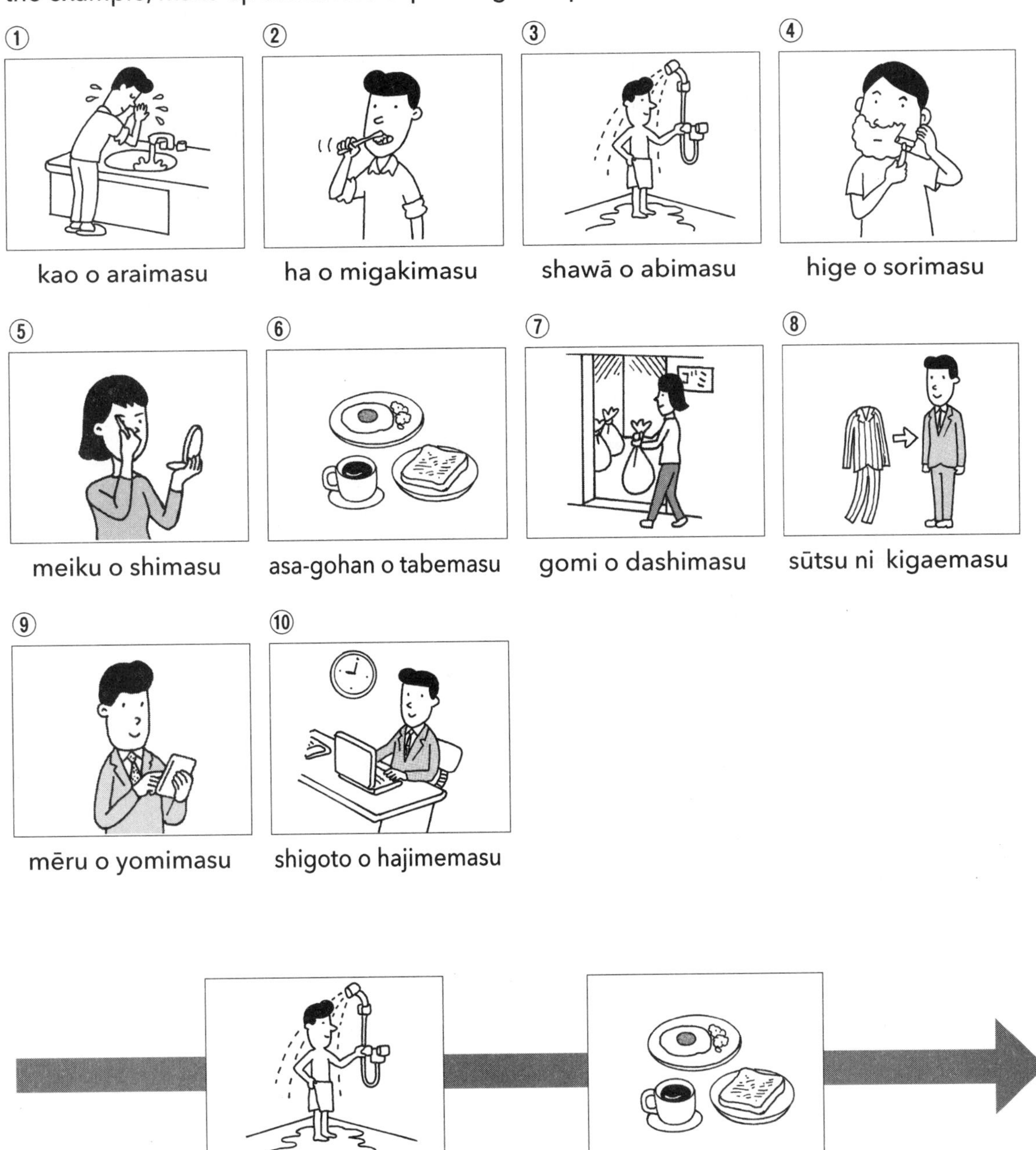

e.g. Watashi wa mainichi asa-gohan o taberu mae ni shawā o abimasu.

VOCABULARY

kao	face	sorimasu	shave	sūtsu	suit
ha	tooth	meiku o shimasu	put on make-up	kigaemasu (R2)	change [clothes]
migakimasu	brush	gomi	trash		
hige	beard	dashimasu	put out		

PRACTICE ②

Make up sentences following the pattern of the example and based on the information provided.

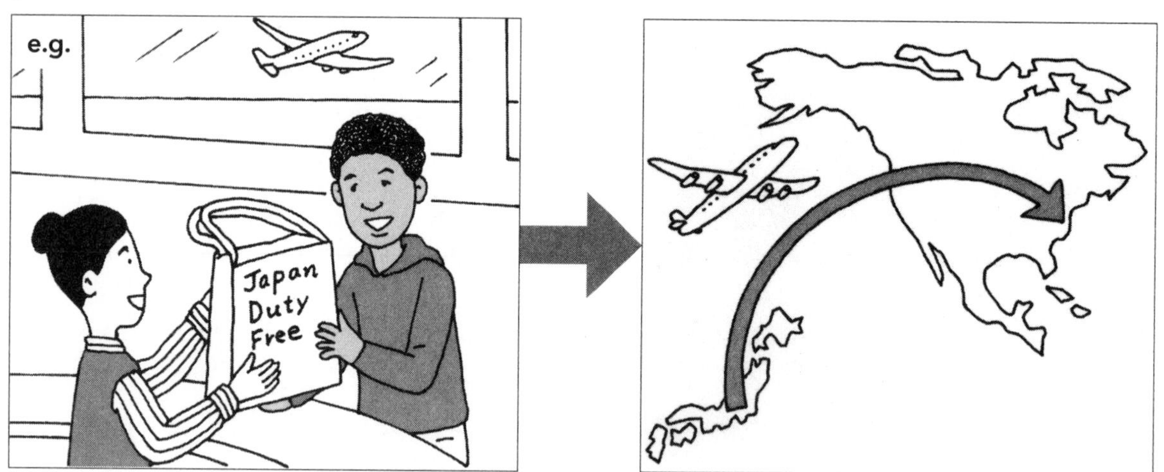

e.g. Pōru-san wa kuni ni kaeru mae ni o-miyage o kaimashita.

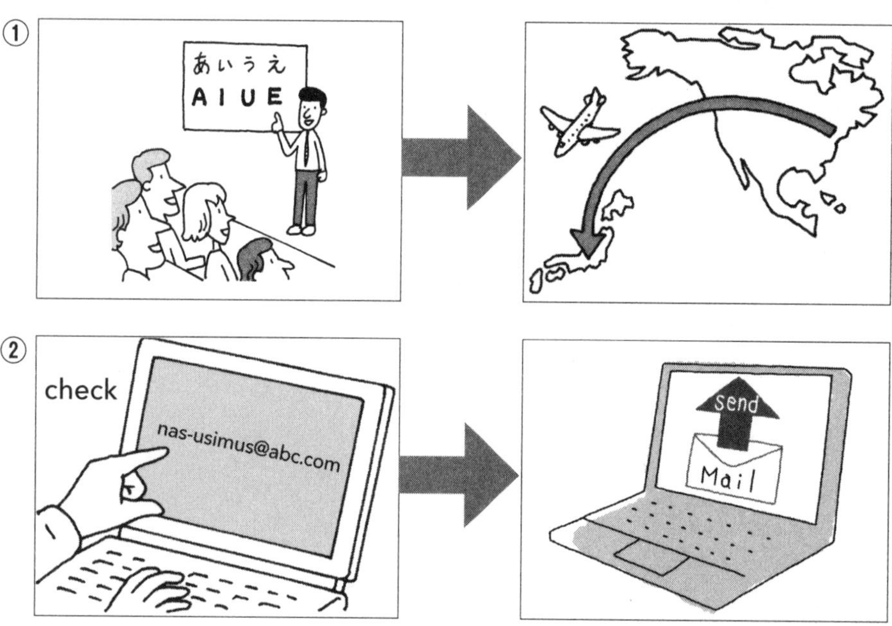

PRACTICE ③

102

Listen to the audio while looking at the illustration. Then practice by substituting the underlined words with words shown in the illustrations below.

Sumisu: [1] **Nihon-go o benkyōshitai desu. Kono chikaku ni ii gakkō ga arimasu ka.**
Suzuki: [2] **Ee, AJALT Sukūru ga ii desu yo.**

①
learn karate dojo

Minato Karate Dōjō

②
view cherry blossoms place

Sakura Kōen

③
buy old furniture shop

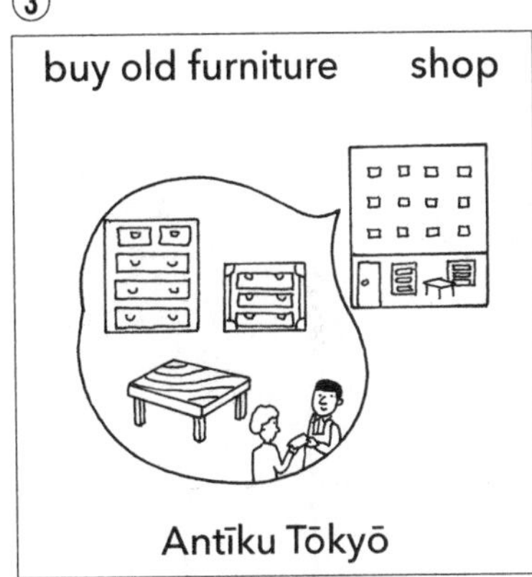

Antīku Tōkyō

VOCABULARY

Minato Karate Dōjō	Minato Karate Dojo (fictitious facility name)
dōjō	dojo

SPEAKING PRACTICE ①

103, 104

Listen to the audio while looking at the illustrations and complete the dialogue.
An event ended, and Suzuki takes Paul back to the hotel.

Suzuki: [1] Sui-yōbi no yoru wa isogashii desu ka.
Pōru: [2] Iie, isogashikunai desu.
Suzuki: [3] (   )
Pōru: [4] Ii desu ne. Zehi.
Suzuki: [5] (   )

SPEAKING PRACTICE ②

105, 106

Listen to the audio while looking at the illustrations and complete the dialogue.

Paul and Suzuki are at a Japanese restaurant. A plate of sashimi has been served.

Pōru: [1] Kirei desu ne.

Suzuki: [2] Itadakimasu.

Pōru: [3] Chotto matte kudasai.

[4] (   )

TARGET DIALOGUE

Listen to the audio while looking at the illustrations and complete the dialogue.

Paul and Suzuki are discussing what to do on Sunday.

Pōru: [1] **Otōto mo anime ga suki desu kara, Akihabara de o-miyage o kaitai desu.**
Suzuki: [2] **Sō desu ka.**
[3] (   )
Pōru: [4] **Arigatō gozaimasu.**
Suzuki: [5] **Pōru-san, hoteru wa doko desu ka.**
Pōru: [6] **Shinjuku no Nozomi Hoteru desu.**
Suzuki: [7] (   )
Pōru: [8] **10-ji desu ne. Wakarimashita.**

PRACTICE ①

Fill in the blanks in the chart below with the appropriate word.

	Masu-form	Te-form
go	ikimasu	itte
meet	aimasu	①
buy	kaimasu	②
learn	naraimasu	③
wait	machimasu	④
return, go home	kaerimasu	⑤
send	okurimasu	⑥
run	hashirimasu	⑦
climb	noborimasu	⑧
draw, write	kakimasu	⑨
listen, ask	kikimasu	⑩
walk	arukimasu	⑪
swim	oyogimasu	⑫
read	yomimasu	⑬
drink	nomimasu	⑭
lend	kashimasu	⑮
speak	hanashimasu	⑯
eat	tabemasu	⑰
give	agemasu	⑱
start	hajimemasu	⑲
go to bed	nemasu	⑳
borrow	karimasu	㉑
see, watch	mimasu	㉒
come	kimasu	㉓
do	shimasu	㉔

PRACTICE ②

Make up dialogues following the patterns of the examples and based on the information provided.

1. e.g. Suzuki: Sumisu-san, ashita nani o shimasu ka.
Sumisu: Shibuya ni itte, eiga o mimasu.

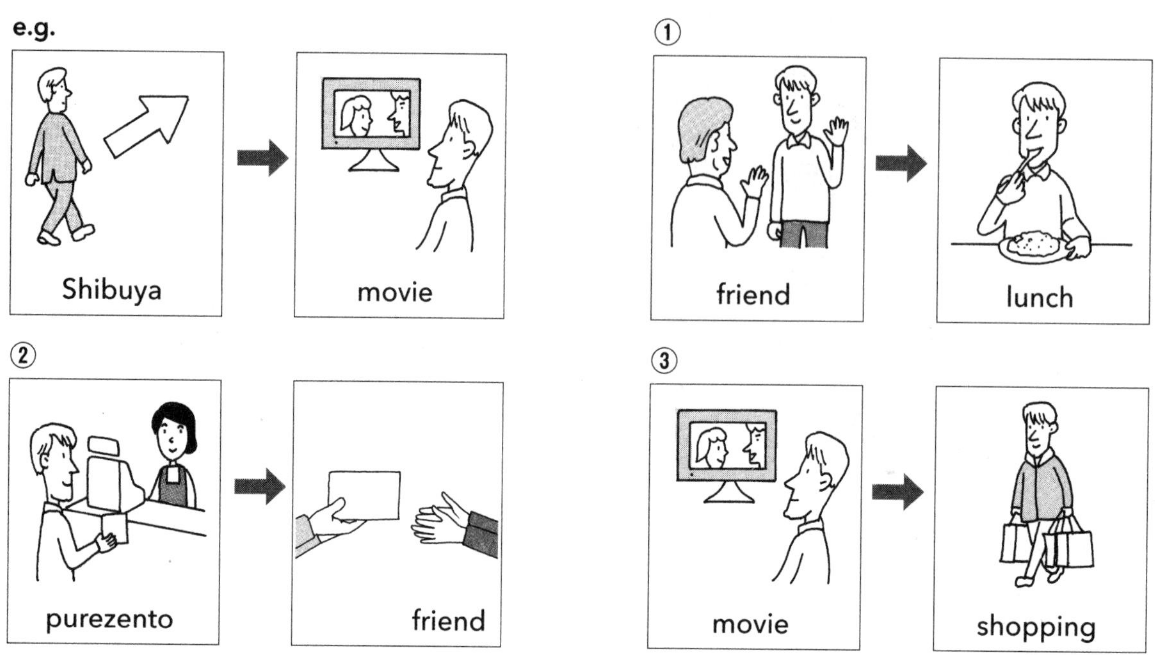

2. e.g. Suzuki: Sumisu-san, kinō nani o shimashita ka.
Sumisu: Toshokan ni itte, hon o yomimashita.

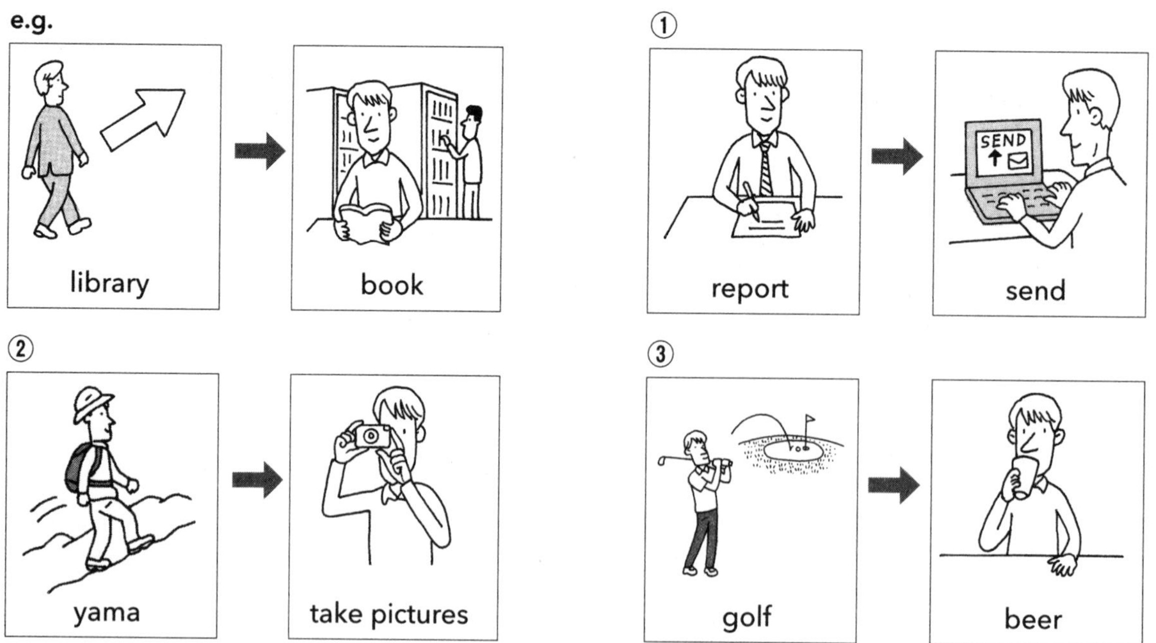

VOCABULARY

purezento	present
yama	mountain

PRACTICE ③

Listen to the audio while looking at the illustration. Then practice by substituting the underlined words with words shown in the illustrations below.

Kato and Smith are talking.

Katō: [1] Sumisu-san, kaigi no ato, nani o shimasu ka.

Sumisu: [2] Kyōto ni itte, o-matsuri o mimasu.

Katō: [3] Sō desu ka.

① 

② 

SPEAKING PRACTICE ①

 110, 111

Make up a dialogue while looking at the illustration. Then listen to the audio and check yourself.

A meeting at the Osaka branch office has ended and Chan comes to talk to Emma.

Chan: [1] **Ema-san, sutēki wa suki desu ka.**

Ema: [2] **Hai, suki desu.**

Chan: [3] **(**   **)**

Ema: [4] **Arigatō gozaimasu.**

[5] **Zehi.**

SPEAKING PRACTICE ②

112,113

Make up a dialogue while looking at the illustration. Then listen to the audio and check yourself.

Smith and Nakamura are talking at the office.

1. from P.M.

2. before? after?

3. after

Sumisu: [1] **Gogo 6-ji kara kaigi ga arimasu.**

[2] ( )

Nakamura: [3] **Kaigi no ato de tabemasu.**

TARGET DIALOGUE

 114, 115

Listen to the audio while looking at the illustrations and complete the dialogue.

Emma speaks to Kato while he is working.

Ema: [1]( )

Katō: [2]Hai.

Ema: [3]( )

Katō: [4]A, pakkēji-fea desu ne.

Ema: [5]( )

[6]Asatte kōjō o mite, 4-ji no hikōki de Tōkyō ni kaerimasu.

Katō: [7]Wakarimashita. Ki o tsukete.

Making a Request: Please Give Her My Regards

PRACTICE ①

Fill in the blanks in the chart below with the appropriate word.

	Masu-form	Te-form		Masu-form	Te-form
say	iimasu	①	show	misemasu	⑥
wait	machimasu	②	stop	tomemasu	⑦
turn	magarimasu	③	tell	oshiemasu	⑧
take	torimasu	④	deliver	todokemasu	⑨
lend	kashimasu	⑤	bring	mottekimasu	⑩

PRACTICE ②

Make up dialogues following the pattern of the example and based on the information provided.

e.g. Katō: [1] **Pen o kashite kudasai.**
Sumisu: [2] **Hai.**

①

②

please wait a moment

③

④

⑤

⑥

⑦

⑧

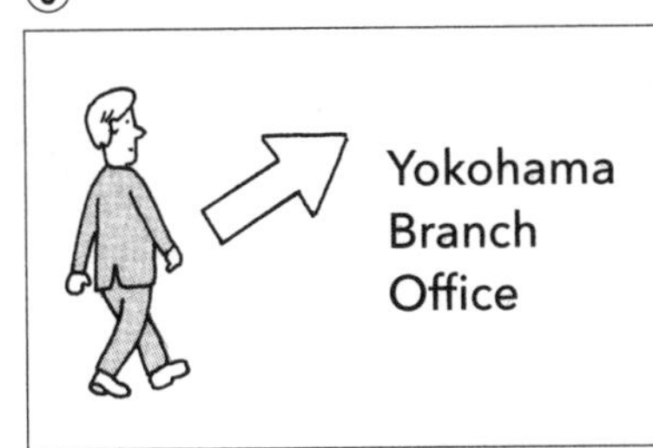

⑨

PRACTICE ③

116

Listen to the audio while looking at the illustrations. Then practice by substituting the underlined words with words shown in the illustrations below.

Smith is in a taxi.

Sumisu: [1] **Shibuya Eki no chikaku made onegaishimasu.**
Untenshu: [2] **Hai.**
Sumisu: [3] **Tsugi no shingō o hidari ni magatte kudasai.**
Untenshu: [4] **Hai.**
Sumisu: [5] **Ano manshon no mae de tomete kudasai.**
Untenshu: [6] **Hai, wakarimashita.**
[7] **4,000-en desu.**
Sumisu: [8] **Hai.**
Untenshu: [9] **Arigatō gozaimashita.**
Sumisu: [10] **Dōmo.**

①
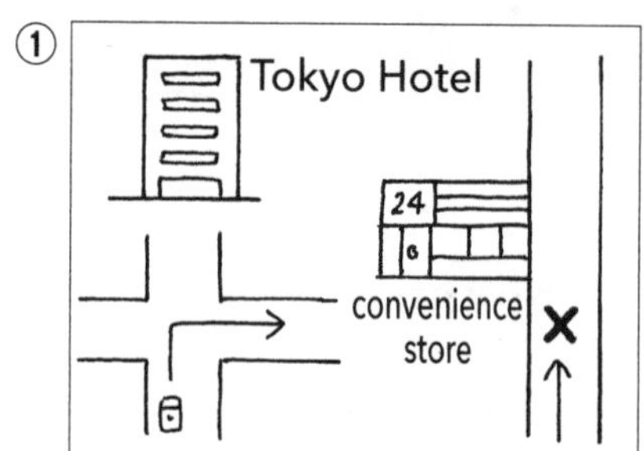

②
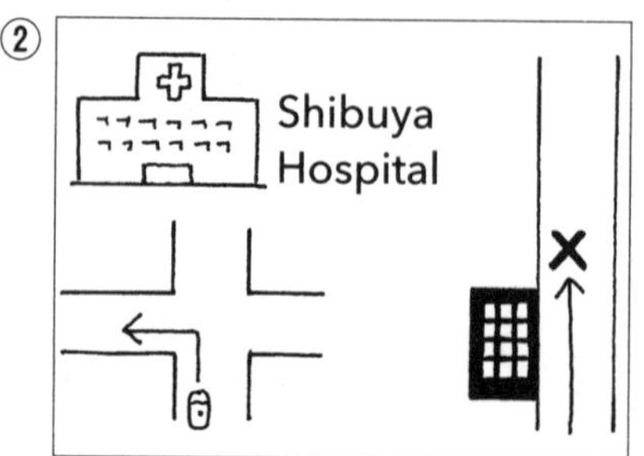

SPEAKING PRACTICE ①

117, 118

Listen to the audio while looking at the illustration and complete the dialogue.

Emma is staying at a hotel.

Hoteru no hito: [1] **Hai, rūmu sābisu desu.**

Ema: [2] ( )

Hoteru no hito: [3] **Hai, shōchishimashita.**

SPEAKING PRACTICE ②

119, 120

Listen to the audio while looking at the illustration and complete the dialogue.

Emma checks out of the hotel.

Ema: [1] ( )

Furonto no hito: [2] **Hai, shōchishimashita.**

TARGET DIALOGUE

 121, 122

Listen to the audio while looking at the illustrations and complete the dialogue.

After the package fair, Emma is in a taxi talking to Kato on the phone.

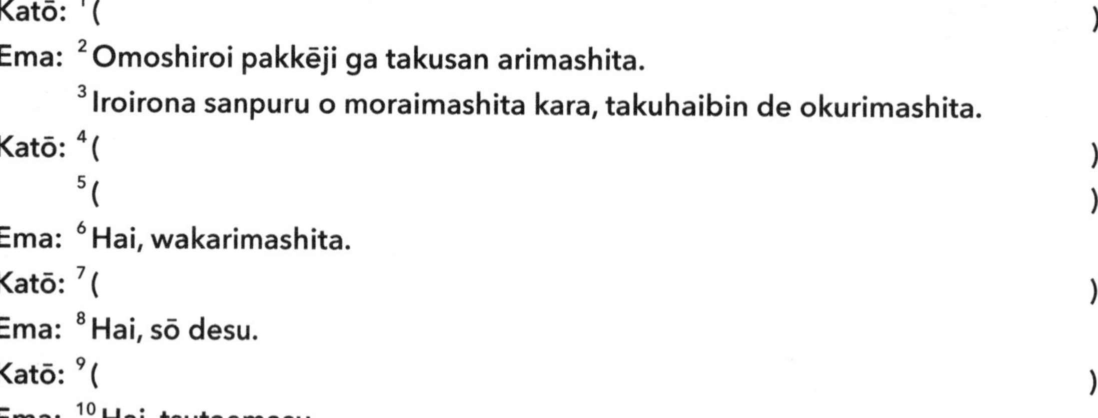

Katō: [1]( )

Ema: [2]Omoshiroi pakkēji ga takusan arimashita.

[3]Iroirona sanpuru o moraimashita kara, takuhaibin de okurimashita.

Katō: [4]( )

[5]( )

Ema: [6]Hai, wakarimashita.

Katō: [7]( )

Ema: [8]Hai, sō desu.

Katō: [9]( )

Ema: [10]Hai, tsutaemasu.

Create a dialogue based on the illustrations.
Smith and Green are at a party.

Do a role play following the instructions below.

[Student A]
You want to go to the beer festival shown below with a friend. You are busy on June 17th and 18th, so you want to go on the 19th or 20th. Ask your friend (Student B) if he/she likes beer and decide the day you will go. You also like modern art. Accept Student B's invitation.

Beer Festival in Hibiya Park

Thursday, June 17	**16:00 – 22:00**
Friday, June 18	**11:00 – 22:00**
Saturday, June 19	**11:00 – 22:00**
Sunday, June 20	**11:00 – 21:00**

Access: Hibiya Station, Exit A10

Bīru Fesutibaru	Beer Festival
Hibiya Kōen	Hibiya Park

[Student B]
You like beer. You are busy on June 18th and 19th, but you have time on the 17th and 20th. Accept the invitation of your friend (Student A). You like modern art as well and you want to go to the exhibition described below. Ask Student A if he/she likes modern art. If the answer is yes, and since Ginza and Hibiya are close by, invite your friend to go to the exhibition before going to the beer festival. Then, decide on where you will meet and what time you will meet.

Modern Art Exhibition in Ginza

Friday, June 11 – Sunday, June 27
10:00 – 20:00

Nozomi Department Store, Ginza Store
Access: Ginza Station, Exit A7

modan-āto	modern art
tenrankai	exhibition
Ginza-ten	Ginza store

LESSON 20 Going Places (3): How Do You Go There?

PRACTICE ①

Make up sentences following the pattern of the example and based on the information provided.

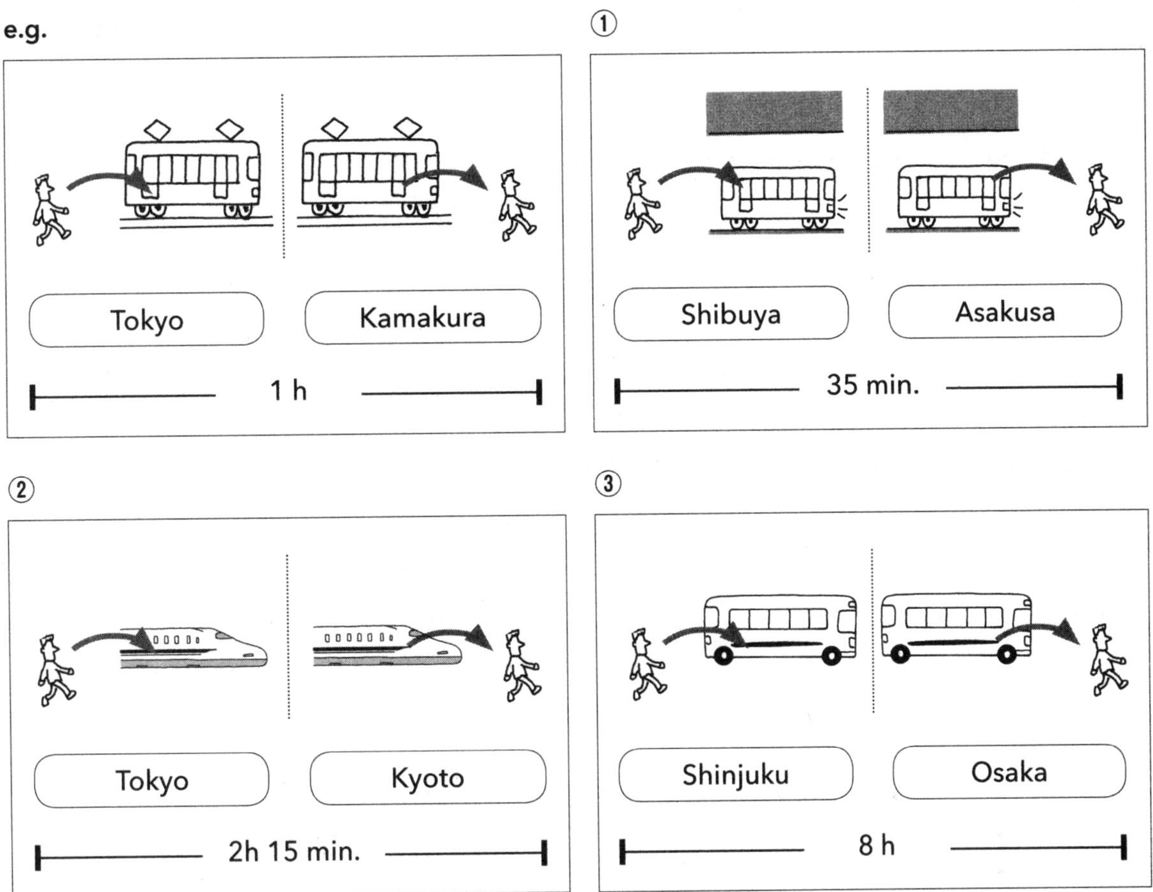

e.g. Sumisu-san wa Tōkyō Eki de densha ni notte, Kamakura Eki de orimashita. Tōkyō Eki kara Kamakura Eki made 1-jikan kakarimashita.

PRACTICE ②

Make up sentences following the pattern of the example and based on the information provided in Smith's itinerary.

Smith climbed Mount Fuji during his summer vacation.

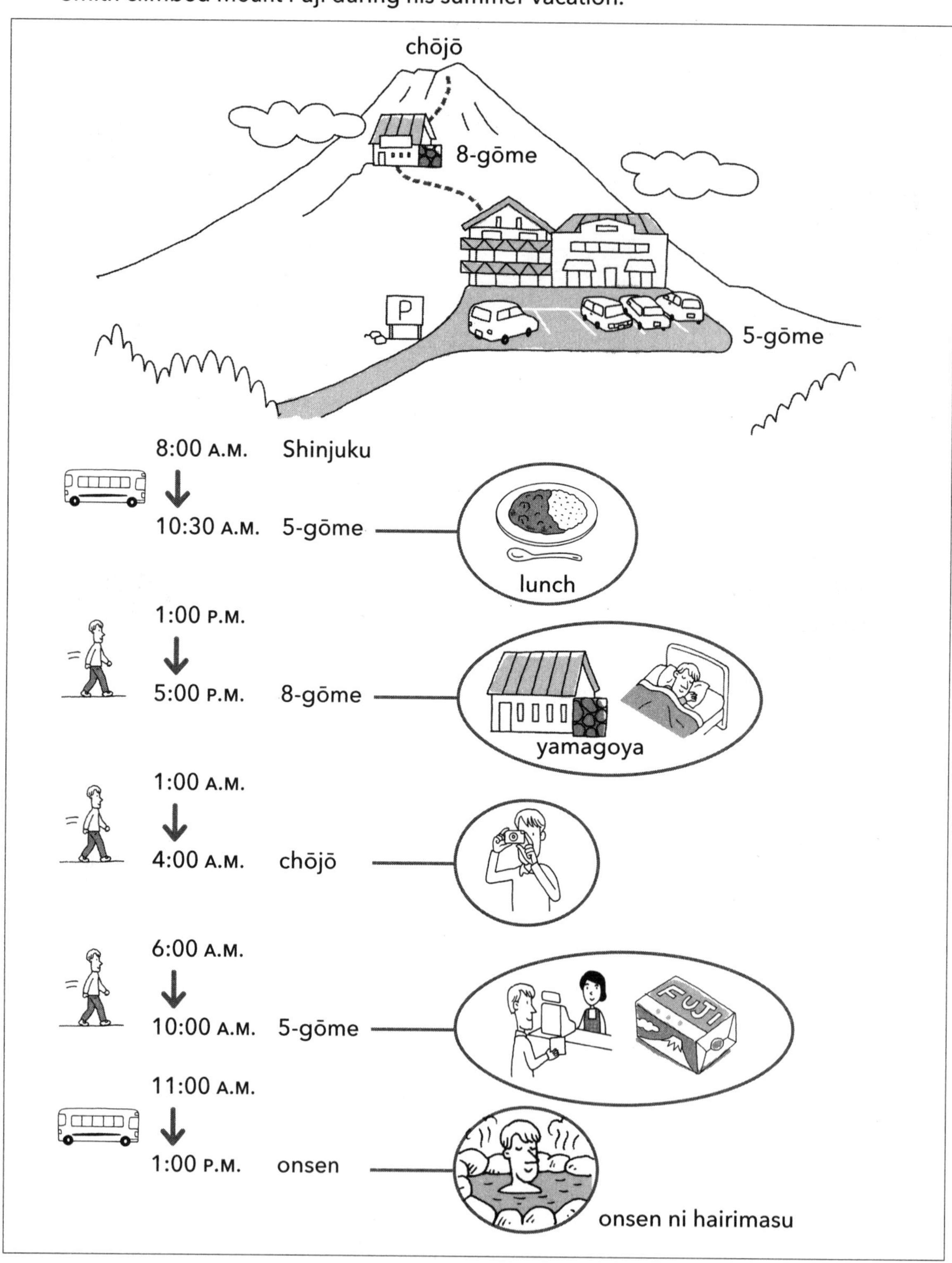

e.g. Sumisu-san wa gozen 8-ji ni Shinjuku de basu ni norimashita.

VOCABULARY

chōjō	peak, summit	**5-gōme**	5th Station	**onsen ni hairimasu**	get into a hot spring
8-gōme	8th Station	**yamagoya**	mountain hut		

PRACTICE ③

123

Look at the illustrations and make up a dialogue. Listen to the audio and check yourself. Then practice by substituting the underlined words with words shown in the illustrations below.

Chan and Suzuki are talking during their break.

1. summer vacation what ?

2. Kyoto

3. I see.

4. how long Kyoto ?

5. 5 days

6. Good!

Chan: [1] Natsu-yasumi ni nani o shimasu ka.

Suzuki: [2] Kyōto ni itte, o-tera o mimasu.

Chan: [3] Sō desu ka.

[4] Donokurai Kyōto ni imasu ka.

Suzuki: [5] Itsuka imasu.

Chan: [6] Ii desu ne.

①

②

SPEAKING PRACTICE

 124, 125

Listen to the audio while looking at the illustration and complete the dialogue.
Paul is at Akihabara Station.

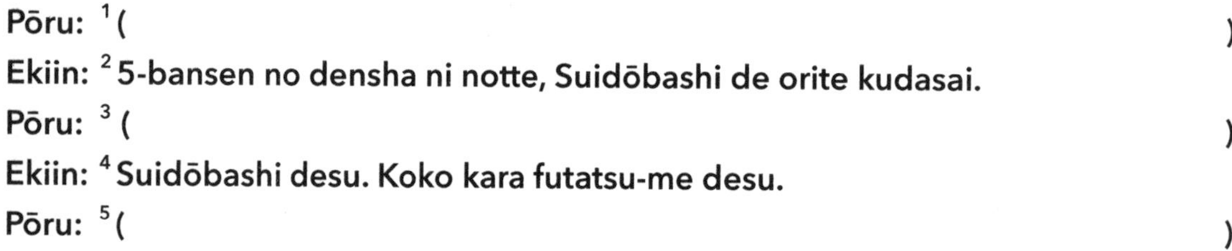

Pōru: 1(   )
Ekiin: 2 5-bansen no densha ni notte, Suidōbashi de orite kudasai.
Pōru: 3(   )
Ekiin: 4 Suidōbashi desu. Koko kara futatsu-me desu.
Pōru: 5(   )

TARGET DIALOGUE

126, 127

Listen to the audio while looking at the illustrations and complete the dialogue.

Smith and Suzuki are meeting at the museum. Smith receives a phone call from Suzuki.

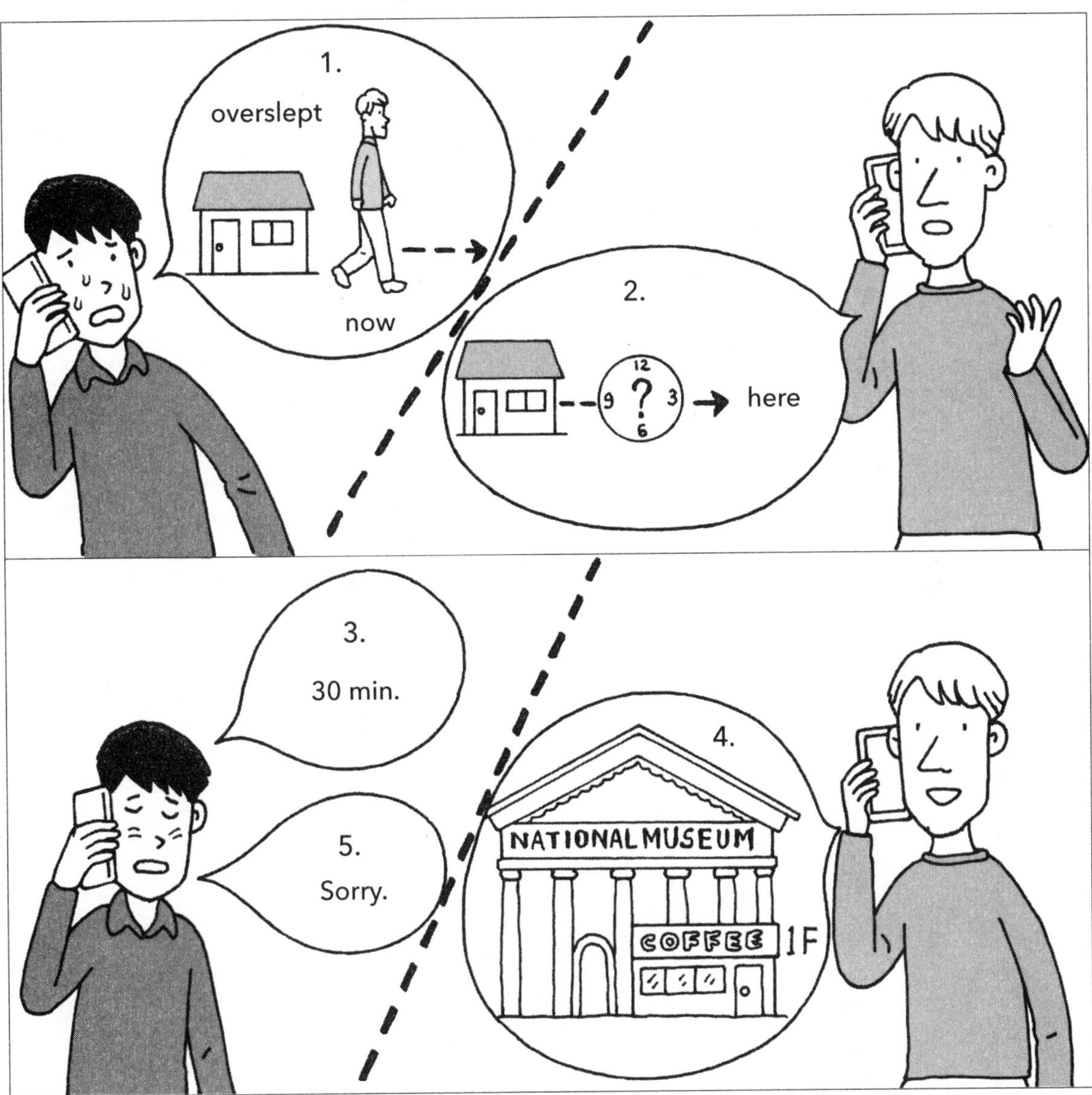

Suzuki: 1 Sumisu-san, sumimasen. Nebōshimashita. Ima uchi o demashita.

Sumisu: 2 ( )

Suzuki: 3 30-pun gurai kakarimasu.

Sumisu: 4 ( )

Suzuki: 5 Sumimasen.

CHALLENGE 4

Make up dialogues following the pattern of the example.

	e.g.	①	②	③	④	⑤
From	Ikebukuro	Ikebukuro	Ikebukuro	Roppongi	Roppongi	Ginza
To	Roppongi	Asakusa	Oshiage (Sukaitsurī-mae)	Shinagawa	Asakusa	Oshiage (Sukaitsurī-mae)

e.g. A: Ikebukuro kara Roppongi ni ikitai desu. Dōyatte ikimasu ka.

B: Ikebukuro de Yamanote-sen ni notte, Ebisu de Hibiya-sen ni norikaete, Roppongi de orite kudasai.

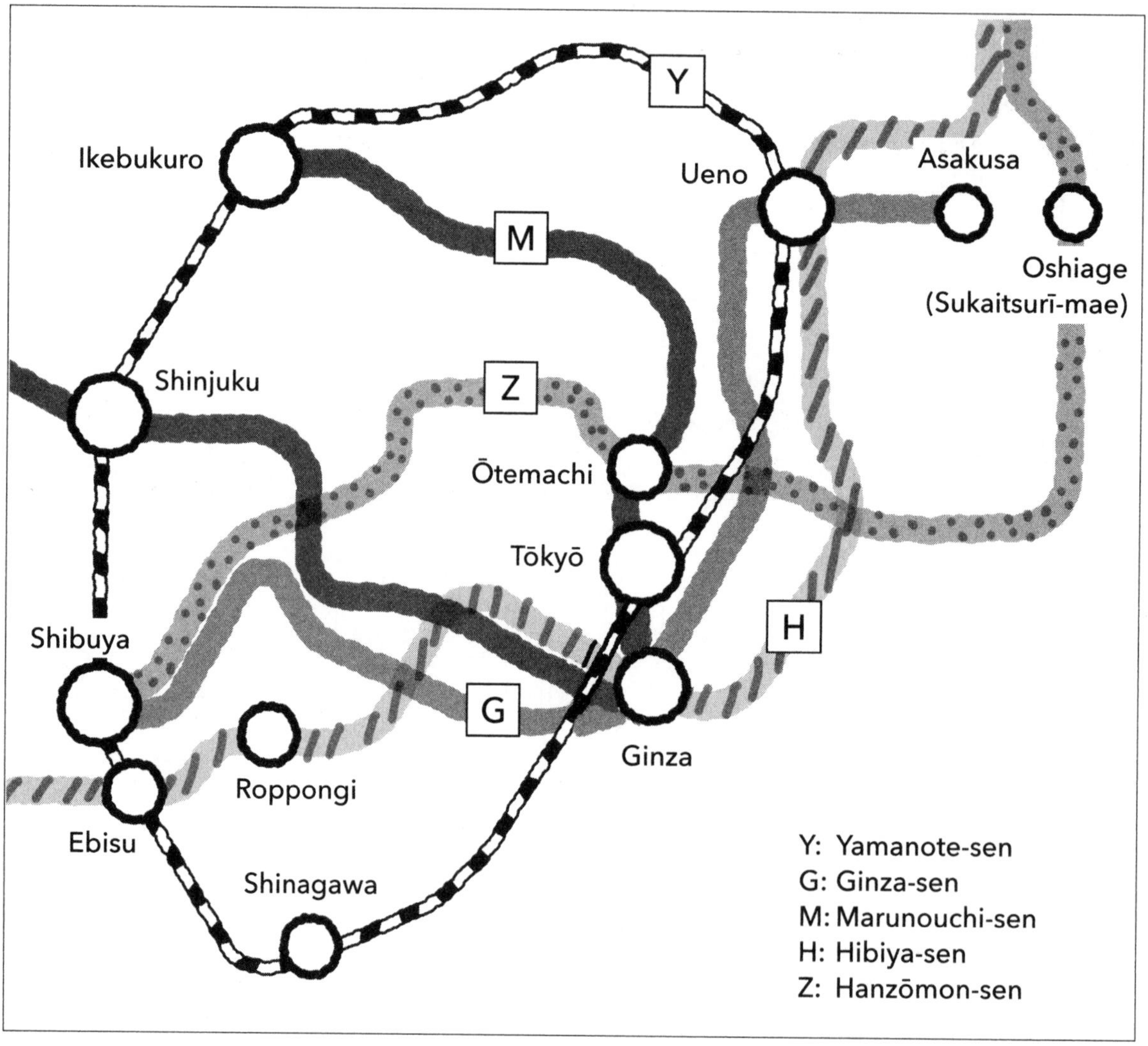

Ikebukuro
Y
Ueno
Asakusa
M
Oshiage
(Sukaitsurī-mae)
Shinjuku
Z
Ōtemachi
Tōkyō
H
Shibuya
G
Ginza
Roppongi
Ebisu
Shinagawa

Y: Yamanote-sen
G: Ginza-sen
M: Marunouchi-sen
H: Hibiya-sen
Z: Hanzōmon-sen

VOCABULARY

Ikebukuro	Ikebukuro (district in Tokyo)
Oshiage	Oshiage (district in Tokyo)
Sukaitsurī	Tokyo Skytree
Yamanote-sen	Yamanote Line
-sen	line
Hibiya-sen	Hibiya Line
norikaemasu (R2)	change trains, transfer
Ueno	Ueno (district in Tokyo)
Shinagawa	Shinagawa (district in Tokyo)
Ginza-sen	Ginza Line
Marunouchi-sen	Marunouchi Line
Hanzōmon-sen	Hanzomon Line

PRACTICE ①

Select the word of the options below that fits into the sentence.

e.g. ① ② ③ ④

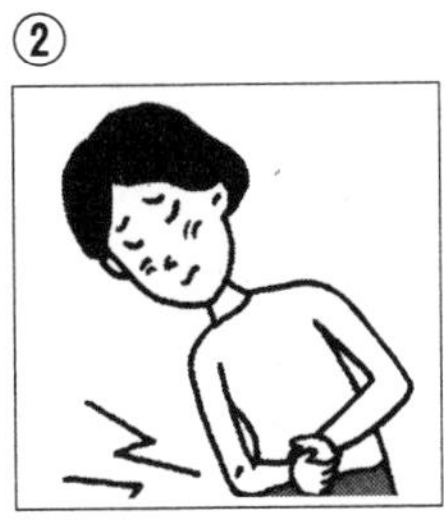

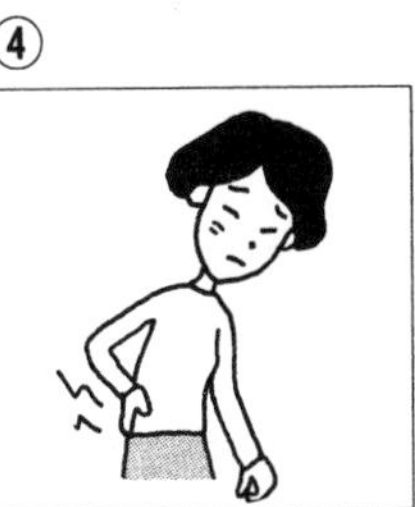

e.g. Kinō o-sake o takusan nomimashita. <u>Atama</u> ga itai desu.
① Chokorēto o takusan tabemashita. (   ) ga itai desu.
② Kinō furui miruku o nomimashita. (   ) ga itai desu.
③ Karaoke de 5-jikan utaimashita. (   ) ga itai desu.
④ Omoi kaban o mochimashita. (   ) ga itai desu.

nodo	onaka	ha	~~atama~~	me	ashi	koshi

PRACTICE ②

Make up sentences following the pattern of the example and based on the information provided.

You have been invited to your friend's house. Ask your friend if you can do something.

e.g.

①

②

③

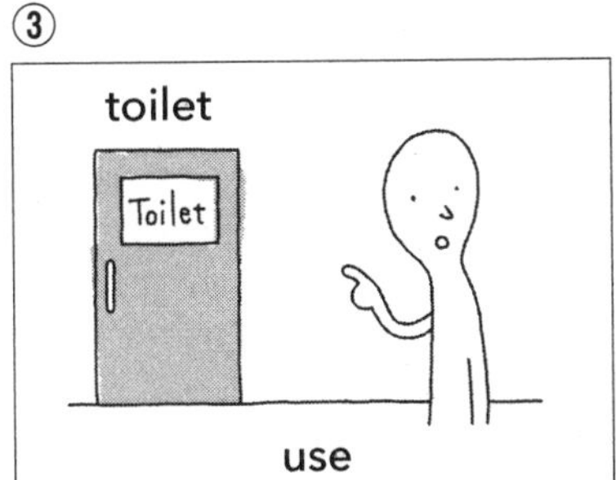

④

⑤

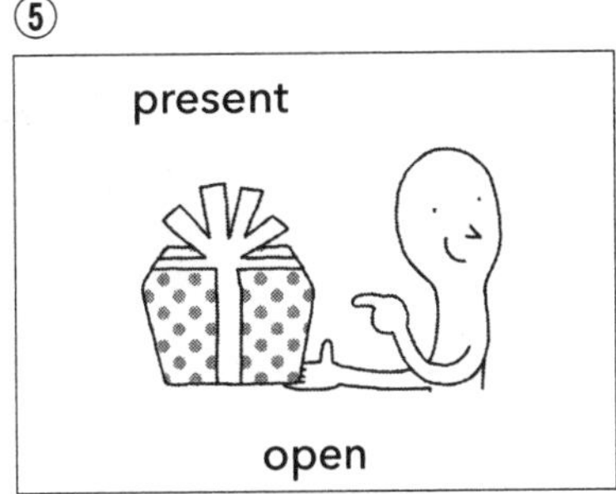

e.g. Arubamu o mite mo ii desu ka.

VOCABULARY

miruku	milk	omoi	heavy	arubamu	album
karaoke	karaoke	mochimasu	carry	kurisumasu-tsurī	Christmas tree

PRACTICE ③

128

Listen to the audio while looking at the illustration. Then practice by substituting the underlined words with words shown in the illustrations below.

Smith is talking to the receptionist.

Sumisu: [1] **Sumimasen. Kaigi-shitsu de o-bentō o tabete mo ii desu ka.**

Uketsuke no hito: [2] **Hai, dōzo.**

Sumisu: [3] **1-ji han made tsukatte mo ii desu ka.**

Uketsuke no hito: [4] **Hai, dōzo.**

①

②

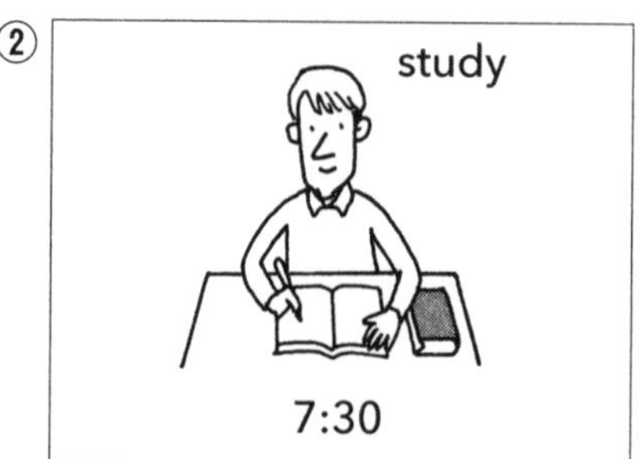

SPEAKING PRACTICE ①

129, 130

Listen to the audio while looking at the illustrations and complete the dialogue.
Green is at the home appliances store.

Gurīn: 1(　　　　)
Mise no hito: 2 Hai, koko ni go-jūsho to o-namae o onegaishimasu.
Gurīn: 3(　　　　)
Mise no hito: 4 Hai.

SPEAKING PRACTICE ②

131,132

Listen to the audio while looking at the illustration and complete the dialogue.
Green is at the clinic.

1.
?

2.
English OK?

3.
OK

Isha: [1] **Dō shimashita ka.**

Gurīn: [2] **(**   **)**

Isha: [3] **Hai, dōzo.**

TARGET DIALOGUE

133,134

Listen to the audio while looking at the illustrations and complete the dialogue.
Smith and Suzuki are at the museum.

1. coins a long time ago ?
2.
3. English Pamphlet
4.
5. OK?
6.
7. tired
8.
9. legs hurt
10. OK?
11.

Sumisu:	**[1] Kore wa mukashi no o-kane desu ka.**
Suzuki:	**[2] Ee, sō desu.**
	[3] A, koko ni Eigo no panfuretto ga arimasu yo.
Sumisu:	**[4] Sō desu ne.**
	[5] ( )
Hakubutsukan no hito:	**[6] Hai, dōzo.**
Suzuki:	**[7] Tsukaremashita ne.**
Sumisu:	**[8] Sō desu ne. [9] ( )**
	[10] ( )
Hakubutsukan no hito:	**[11] Hai, dōzo.**

PRACTICE ①

Fill in the blanks in the chart below with the appropriate word.

	Masu-form	Nai-form
go	ikimasu	ikanai
buy	kaimasu	①
wash	araimasu	②
use	tsukaimasu	③
wait	machimasu	④
stand up	tachimasu	⑤
return, go home	kaerimasu	⑥
run	hashirimasu	⑦
take	torimasu	⑧
touch	sawarimasu	⑨
write, draw	kakimasu	⑩
put, place	okimasu	⑪
swim	oyogimasu	⑫
read	yomimasu	⑬
turn off	keshimasu	⑭
speak, talk	hanashimasu	⑮
eat	tabemasu	⑯
open	akemasu	⑰
teach, tell	oshiemasu	⑱
turn on	tsukemasu	⑲
show	misemasu	⑳
see, watch	mimasu	㉑
put in, add	iremasu	㉒
come	kimasu	㉓
do	shimasu	㉔

PRACTICE ②

135

Following the pattern of the example, make up sentences by choosing information from B that fits with information from A.

A:

e.g. Kin'en desu.

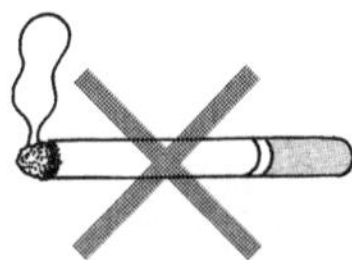

① Chūsha-kinshi desu.

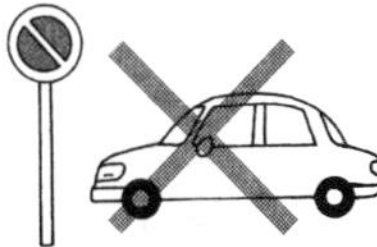

② Tachiiri-kinshi desu.

③ Kono gyūnyū wa furui desu.

④ Kono isu wa kitanai desu.

B:

e.g. Kin'en desu kara, tabako o suwanaide kudasai.

VOCABULARY

gyūnyū	milk
kitanai	dirty

PRACTICE ③

136

Look at the illustrations and make up a dialogue. Listen to the audio and check yourself. Then practice by substituting the underlined words with words shown in the illustrations below.

Smith is placing an order in a shop.

1.

2.
Yes sir.

3.

4.
OK,
I understand.

Sumisu: [1] Hanbāgā o onegaishimasu.

Mise no hito: [2] Hai.

Sumisu: [3] Sumimasen ga, tomato o irenaide kudasai.

Mise no hito: [4] Hai, wakarimashita.

①

②

SPEAKING PRACTICE ①

137,138

Listen to the audio while looking at the illustration and complete the dialogue.

Smith got tipsy at Sasaki's house yesterday and spilled red wine on her carpet.

1. Good morning.

3. yesterday sorry

2. Good morning.

4.

Sumisu: [1] Sasaki-san, ohayō gozaimasu.

Sasaki: [2] ( )

Sumisu: [3] Kinō wa sumimasen deshita.

Sasaki: [4] ( )

SPEAKING PRACTICE ②

 139, 140

Listen to the audio while looking at the illustration and complete the dialogue.

Smith has a pain in his stomach and is being examined by a doctor.

1.
today

2.
OK.

Isha: [1] **Kyō wa o-sake o nomanaide kudasai.**

Sumisu: [2] ( )

TARGET DIALOGUE

141, 142

Listen to the audio while looking at the illustrations and complete the dialogue.
Smith and Suzuki are at the museum.

Sumisu: [1]( )

Suzuki: [2]Hontō ni kirei desu ne. Kore wa 300-nen gurai mae no kimono desu.

Sumisu: [3]( )

Hakubutsukan no hito: [4]Sumimasen. Koko de shashin o toranaide kudasai.

Sumisu: [5]( )

Suzuki: [6]Sumisu-san, asoko ni mo kireina kimono ga arimasu yo.

Sumisu: [7]( )

LESSON 23 Explaining Actions: What Are You Doing Now?

PRACTICE ①

Fill in the blanks in the chart below with the appropriate word.

	Masu-form	Te imasu-form	
		aff.	*neg.*
make	tsukurimasu	tsukutte imasu	tsukutte imasen
write	kakimasu	①	②
sleep	nemasu	③	④
learn	naraimasu	⑤	⑥
clean	sōji o shimasu	⑦	⑧
read	yomimasu	⑨	⑩

PRACTICE ②

Make up sentences following the pattern of the example and based on the information provided.

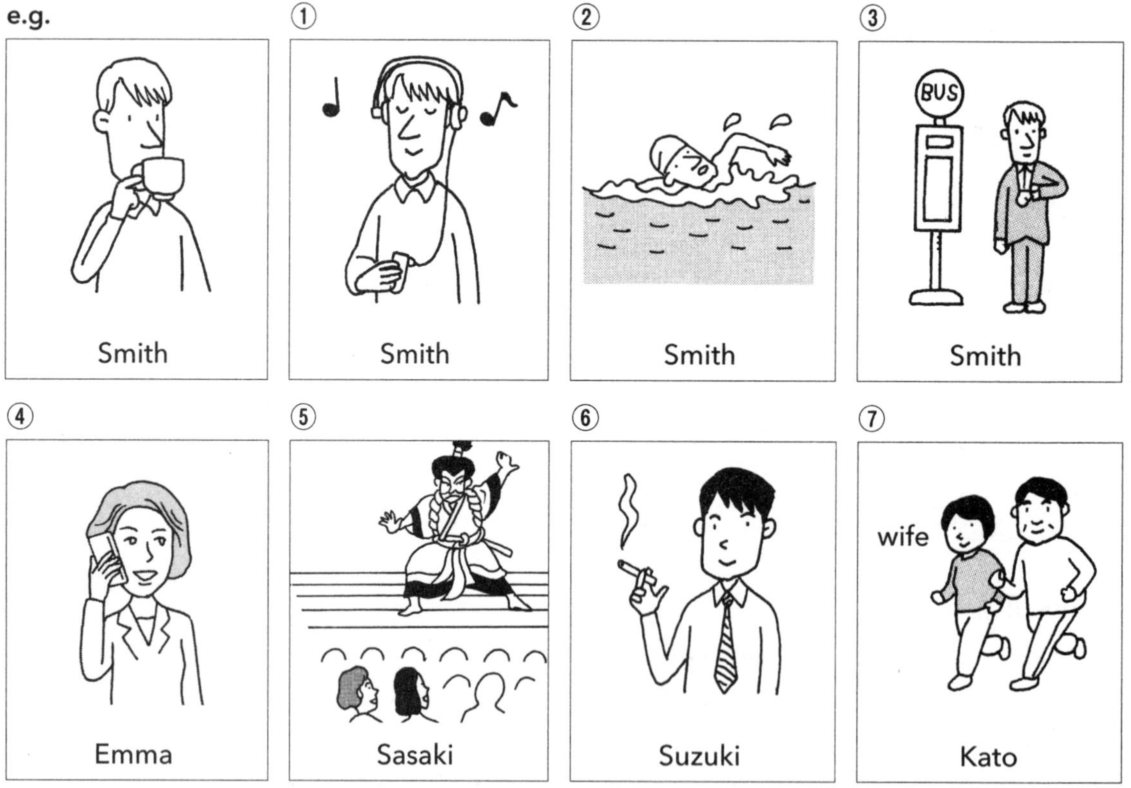

e.g. Sumisu-san wa ima kōhī o nonde imasu.

PRACTICE ③

This page lists the events of one day in Smith's calendar. Pretending you are Smith, answer the questions.
(Note: The question is asked at the time shown in the question box at the right.)

6:30	Okimasu.
7:00–7:20	Asa-gohan o tabemasu.
8:05	Kaisha ni tsukimasu.
8:30–9:30	Nihon-go no benkyō o shimasu.
9:30–10:15	Katō-san to uchiawase o shimasu.
11:30–12:55	Nozomi Depāto no Tanaka-san to 6-kai no kaigi-shitsu de kaigi o shimasu.
13:00–14:00	Nozomi Depāto no Tanaka-san to tonari no resutoran de shokuji o shimasu.
16:00–17:30	Purezen no junbi o shimasu. (shiryō o tsukurimasu.)
18:00	Kaisha o demasu.
18:30	Uchi ni kaette ban-gohan o tsukurimasu.
19:00–20:00	Ban-gohan o tabemasu.
21:00–22:30	Pasokon de eiga o mimasu.
23:00	Nemasu.

e.g. 7:30
Mō asa-gohan o tabemashita ka.
Hai, tabemashita.

① 8:00
Mō kaisha ni tsukimashita ka.

② 10:00
Ima nani o shite imasu ka.

③ 12:00
Mō hiru-gohan o tabemashita ka.

④ 13:30
Ima nani o shite imasu ka.

⑤ 17:00
Mō purezen no junbi wa dekimashita ka.

⑥ 19:00
Mō uchi ni kaerimashita ka.

⑦ 22:00
Ima nani o shite imasu ka.

VOCABULARY

okimasu (R2) get up [in the morning]

PRACTICE ④

143

Listen to the audio while looking at the illustrations. Then practice by substituting the underlined words with words shown in the illustrations below.

Smith is looking for Chan, who is visiting from the Osaka branch office.

1.
2.
4F
3F
meeting room
2F
1F
3.
4.
new product
Tanaka-san
5.
I see.
Thank you.

Sumisu: [1] Suzuki-san, Chan-san wa doko desu ka.
Suzuki: [2] 3-gai no kaigi-shitsu desu.
Sumisu: [3] Sō desu ka.
Suzuki: [4] Ima Nozomi Depāto no Tanaka-san ni atarashii shōhin no setsumei o shite imasu.
Sumisu: [5] Wakarimashita. Arigatō.

①

Chan, café (1F)
with client

②

Nakamura, meeting room (4F)
with eigyō-bu no hito

VOCABULARY

eigyō-bu	sales division

SPEAKING PRACTICE ①

144, 145

Listen to the audio while looking at the illustration and complete the dialogue.

Smith is at the dry cleaners.

Sumisu: [1] **Kore, onegaishimasu.** [2] **(**)

Mise no hito: [3] **Sui-yōbi no yūgata dekimasu.**

SPEAKING PRACTICE ②

146, 147

Listen to the audio while looking at the illustration and complete the dialogue.

On a holiday, Chan calls Emma.

Ema: [1] **Moshi moshi.**

Chan: [2] **Chan desu.** [3] **(**)

Ema: [4] **Sumimasen. Ima ryōri o shite imasu.**

Chan: [5] **(**)

Ema: [6] **Onegaishimasu.**

SPEAKING PRACTICE ③

148, 149

Listen to the audio while looking at the illustration and complete the dialogue.

Kato and Smith are talking during their break.

1.

?

sometimes

2.

3.

after work?

4.

No.

in the morning

Katō: [1] Sumisu-san, nanika undō o shite imasu ka.

Sumisu: [2] ( )

Katō: [3] Shigoto no ato desu ka.

Sumisu: [4] ( )

TARGET DIALOGUE

150, 151

Listen to the audio while looking at the illustrations and complete the dialogue.

Kato has asked Smith to prepare for a meeting.

1. ready?

2. Sorry not yet.

3.

4. finish by 3 ?

5. Yes soon

15 minutes later

6. materials done

7. Check please.

8.

Katō: [1] **Mō kaigi no junbi wa dekimashita ka.**

Sumisu: [2] **Sumimasen. Mada desu.**

[3] (   )

Katō: [4] **Sō desu ka. 3-ji made ni owarimasu ka.**

Sumisu: [5] (   )

Sumisu: [6] (   )

[7] (   )

Katō: [8] **Hai.**

LESSON 24 Work and Interests: I Work for an Apparel Maker

PRACTICE ①

This is Smith's family. Pretending you are Smith, introduce his family members following the example given.

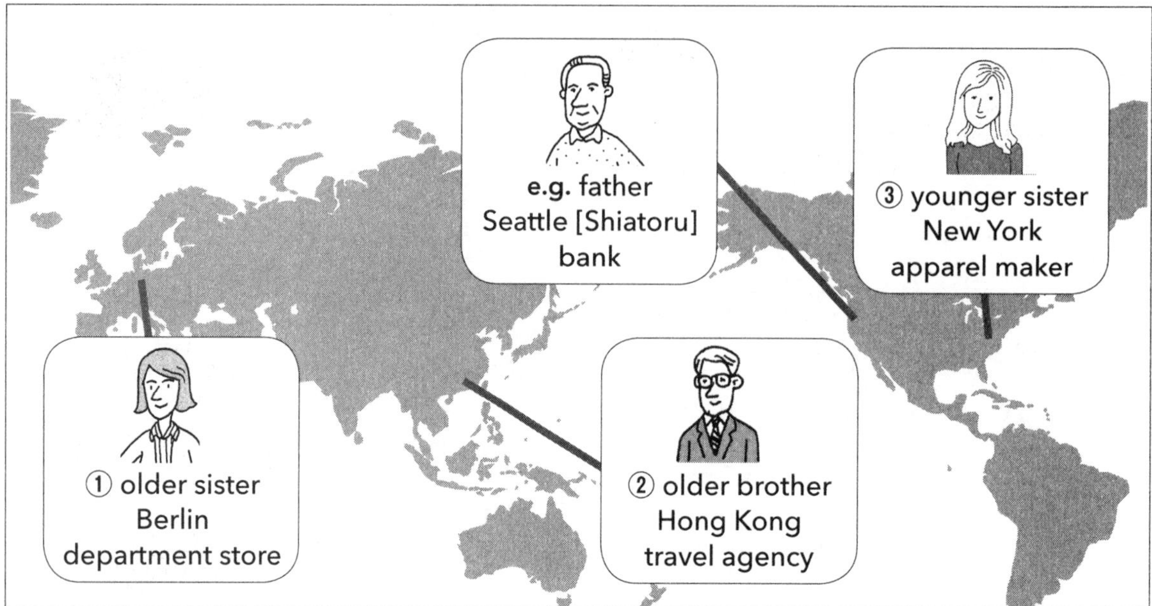

e.g. Chichi wa Shiatoru ni sunde imasu.
Ginkō ni tsutomete imasu.

PRACTICE ②

Make up sentences following the pattern of the example and based on the information provided.

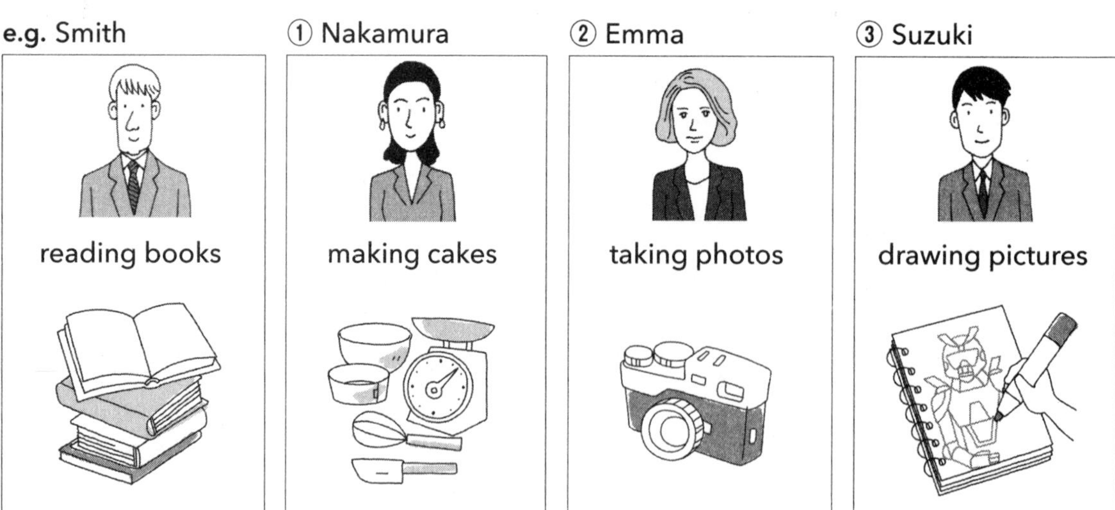

e.g. Sumisu-san no shumi wa hon o yomu koto desu.

VOCABULARY

Shiatoru	Seattle

PRACTICE ③

152

Listen to the audio while looking at the illustrations. Then practice by substituting the underlined words with words shown in the illustrations below.

Chan wants to know Ando's contact information.

1. Ando JBP Japan know ?

2. Yes.

3. know ? xx-xxxx-xxxx

4. sorry

Chan: [1] **JBP Japan no Andō-san o shitte imasu ka.**

Suzuki: [2] **Hai, shitte imasu.**

Chan: [3] **Ja, Andō-san no denwa-bangō o shitte imasu ka.**

Suzuki: [4] **Sumimasen. Wakarimasen.**

①

②
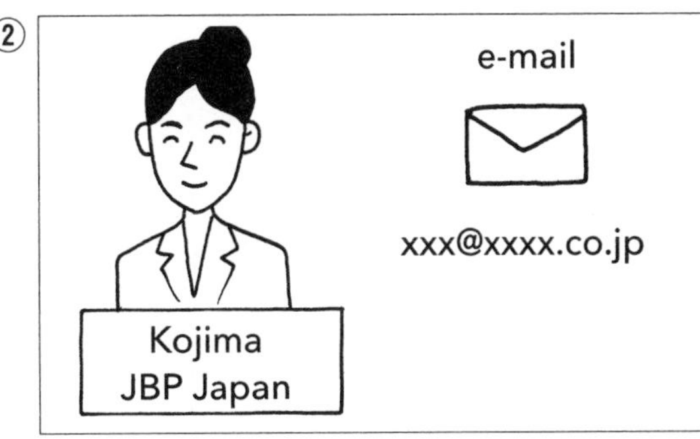

SPEAKING PRACTICE ①

 153, 154

Listen to the audio while looking at the illustrations and complete the dialogue.
Kato is talking with Raja.

1. University of Tokyo

2. Yes.

3. ? specialty

4. biotechnology

5. Prof. Mori know ?

6. Yes.

Katō: [1]( )
Raja: [2]Hai.
Katō: [3]( )
Raja: [4]Baiotekunorojī desu.
Katō: [5]( )
Raja: [6]Hai, yoku shitte imasu.

SPEAKING PRACTICE ②

155, 156

Listen to the audio while looking at the illustration and complete the dialogue.

Smith wants to call Tanaka right away.

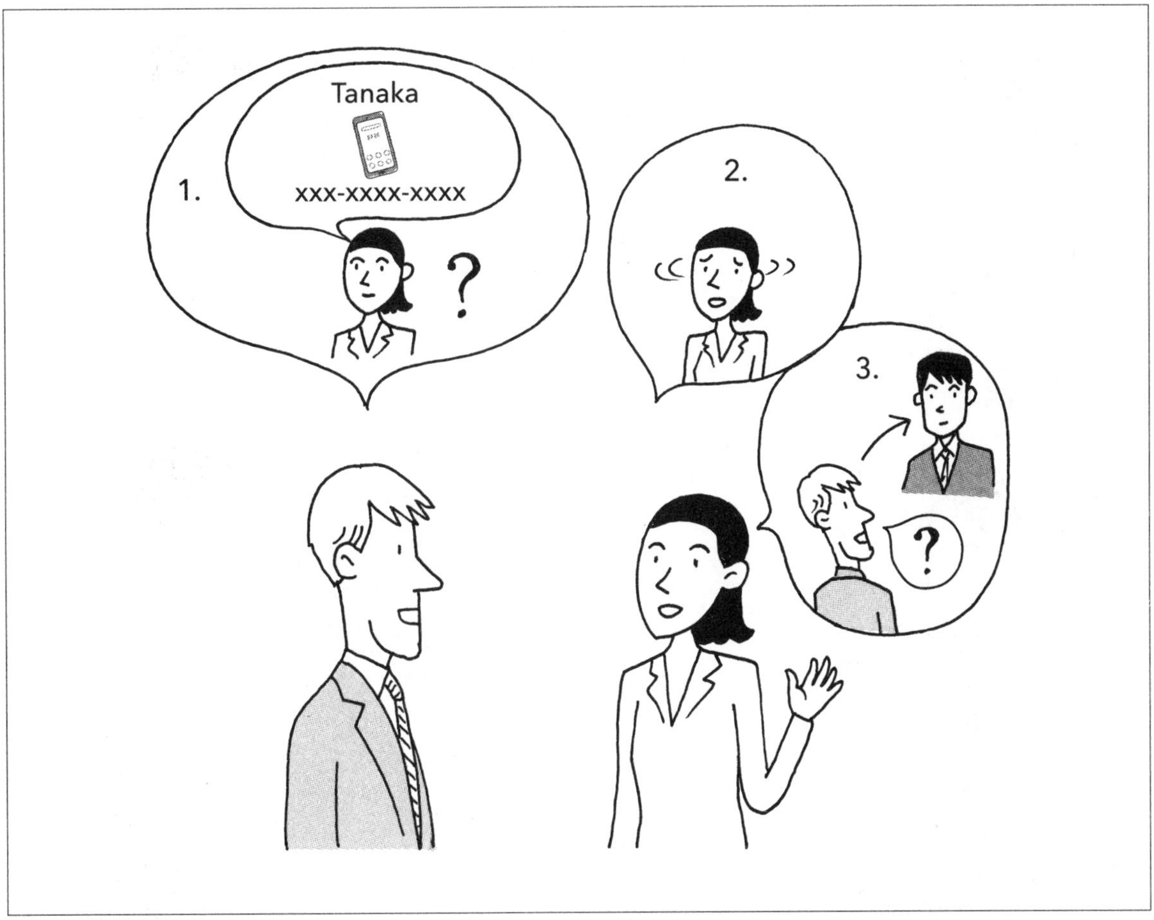

Sumisu: [1] **Nakamura-san,Tanaka-san no keitai no bangō o shitte imasu ka.**

Nakamura: [2] ( )

[3] ( )

TARGET DIALOGUE

 157, 158

Listen to the audio while looking at the illustrations and complete the dialogue.

The staff of the office are together at an *izakaya* drinking place. Smith's younger sister Lisa, who is visiting Japan, joins them.

Suzuki: [1] **Sumisu-san, imōto-san wa Nihongo ga wakarimasu ka.**

Sumisu: [2] **Hai, sukoshi wakarimasu yo.**

Suzuki: [3] **Risa-san, o-shigoto wa?**

Risa: [4] ( )

[5] ( )

Suzuki: [6] **O-shigoto wa tanoshii desu ka.**

Risa: [7] **Ee, totemo tanoshii desu.**

[8] ( )

Suzuki: [9] **Sō desu ka. Ganbatte kudasai.**

Risa: [10] ( )

REVIEW 5

Create a dialogue based on the illustrations.
Chan and Nakamura are at the art museum.

VOCABULARY

furasshu	[camera] flash

COMPREHENSIVE REVIEW

Imagine that you are visiting the house of a Japanese friend. (Make one up if you don't have one in real life.)

1. You meet your friend's family for the first time. Greet the family and introduce yourself.

2. Give the family a gift. Be sure to use appropriate gift-giving expressions.

3. Tell the family about your job—what you do, where you work, etc.—and where you live.

4. Tell the family about your daily routine and what your interests are.

5. Ask the family what their interests are and what they typically do on weekends.

6. At the dinner table, praise the food you have been served.

7. Having been asked what your favorite sports are, explain.

8. Tell the family where you are from and talk about the products or places that your hometown is famous for.

9. Talk about your family—how many members are in it, what they do and where they live.

10. Tell the family that it is time for you to get going, and thank them for their hospitality.

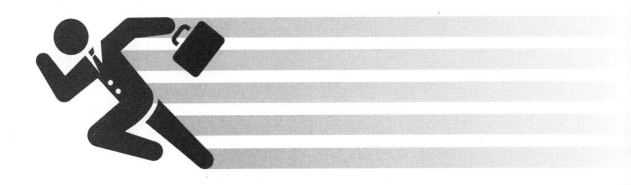